MOTIVATION

A TOOL to enhance efficiency and achieve progress

Rupal Jain

PUSTAK MAHAL

Publishers
Pustak Mahal®

Administrative office and sale centre

J-3/16 , Daryaganj, New Delhi-110002
☎ 23276539, 23272783, 23272784 • *Fax:* 011-23260518
E-mail: info@pustakmahal.com • *Website:* www.pustakmahal.com

Branches
Bengaluru: ☎ 080-22234025 • *Telefax:* 080-22240209
E-mail: pustakmahalblr@gmail.com
Mumbai: ☎ 022-22010941, 022-22053387
E-mail: unicornbooksmumbai@gmail.com
Patna: ☎ 0612-3294193 • *Telefax:* 0612-2302719
E-mail: rapidexptn@gmail.com

ISBN 978-81-223-1324-6

Edition: 2016

Price : ₹ 195/-

Printed at : Radha Offset, Delhi

PREFACE

It gives me immense pleasure to present this edition of the book on *Motivation – A tool to enhance efficiency and achieve progress.*

I have tried to present the subject in a simple manner. A number of examples and anecdotes are included which will help the readers further.

I hope this book will help the readers in understanding various tools of motivation which in turn will increase their productivity and efficiency.

Suggestions for improvement from readers are welcome. For further queries and explanations you can contact me at jainrupal@sify.com

To my daughter SACHIKA for her unconditional love and support.

Contents

MOTIVATION – AN OVERVIEW

"The only way to get people to enjoy working is by motivating them. Today, people must understand the reason why they should work hard. Every individual in an organization is motivated by something different."

—Rick Pitino

In any organization, a **motivated** employee always produces optimal result. So, what is **motivation**?

The word motivation is derived from the word "motive", which find its origin in the Latin word "movere", meaning to "move". Flippo defines **motivation** as a process of attempting to influence others to do their will through the possibility of gain or rewards. According to some experts, it is the drive that propels individuals to behave in a specific manner. Motivation encourages employees to willingly contribute and work productively toward achieving the organizational goal. Thus, it aims at a "win-win" situation for the employee as well as the employer which results in a cordial labour-management relation.

W.G. Scot believes that motivation is a process of stimulating people to take action to accomplishing the desired goals. Motivation inspires, encourages, and promotes mutual trust, cooperation, and unity among employees. It generates the desire, the drive, the spark and the willingness to perform a task efficiently. It raises their morale and stimulates them to work with zeal and enthusiasm. Research has revealed that there is direct relationship between motivation and achievement. Thus, it's an ongoing, repetitive, continuous and core function of management.

"Management is nothing more than motivating other people."

—Lee Iacocca

An effective manager should create a congenial work environment to accomplish organizational objectives. A pleasant surrounding requires cohesion of individual efforts for which managers need to continuously motivate their employees. However, the intensity of motivation varies at different ranks (lower/middle/upper), different times; both within and between employees.

Thus, the biggest challenge for any manager is not only attracting skilled and talented workforce but also retaining them. However, a motivational tool for one employee may be a demotivating factor for another.

A "Thank You" note, a letter or a few words of appreciation can be high motivators for some employees, but not all. For others, money can be an important motivating factor. As Michael J. Jucius feels, "*Motivation is the act of stimulating someone or oneself to get a desired course of action, to push the right button to get a desired result*".

Theories of Motivation

Over the years, different **theories of motivation** have been identified and analyzed by various experts. The theories of motivation can be classified into traditional and modern theories.

5 Traditional Theories

1. **Be Strong Theory**: Also known as the "Fear and Punishment Theory", it is usually adopted by an autocratic manager who leads his followers, takes decisions and expects them to implement his orders without asking "why".
2. **Monastic Theory:** This theory states that money is the only motivational factor for its employees.
3. **Carrot and Stick Theory:** This theory assumes that employees perform efficiently if motivated by rewards such as incentives, perks, bonus with a blend of punishment such as demotion, removal, etc.

4. **Efforts and Rewards Theory:** This theory stresses on piece-rate system of wage-payment to monitor the performance of each employee.

5. **Paternalistic Theory:** This theory suggests that like parents are towards their children, an employer must be kind and generous towards his employees.

10 Modern Theories

Changing times, modern concepts on motivation have been introduced by various analysts. Some of these theories are:

1. **Need Hierarchy Theory of Motivation:** This theory identifies five basic human needs viz – physiological/biological needs, safety/security needs, social needs, esteem needs and self-actualization needs.

   Dr. Abraham Maslow (1908-1970), an American personality theorist in 1973 suggested the theory of human motivation. Maslow identified five sets of human needs which are arranged in a particular order, in a hierarchy of their importance and priority to individuals. He stated that when one set of need is satisfied, the next need in the hierarchy takes its position.

   Maslow recognised five basic human needs which constitute a hierarchy:

   Level 1: **Physiological/biological needs:** They are the basic or primary needs for the survival of human beings. It includes food, air, water, sleep, shelter and sexual satisfaction. These powerful motivators are important for man to survive. If these basic needs are left unsatisfied, other needs will not emerge. These needs lie at the lowest level in the hierarchy since they cannot be prolonged.

   Level 2: **Security/Safety needs:** These are the needs for self-protection and financial autonomy. Employees need job safety, security, and provision for old age insurance, etc. These needs are connected with the psychological fear of loss of job, property, natural calamities, and work vulnerability. An organization can satisfy these needs through pension plan, job security, medical insurance, life insurance schemes, etc.

   Level 3: **Social needs:** Man is a social animal and hence feel the need to belong to a group, association or community. All human beings desire to belong to some group and expect to be accepted with love, respect, affection and recognition. Organizations can organize picnics, get-togethers, parties, cultural and sports activities to satisfy the social need of employees.

Level 4: Esteem needs: Once the other needs are satisfied, an individual feels that he should be respected and appreciated by others. They include attributes such as self-assurance, self-esteem, authority, status, triumph, honour and position. The organization can provide better status, job designation, recognition, appreciation by superiors to satisfy an individual's esteem needs.

Level 5: Self-actualization needs: This is at the top of the hierarchy of needs. Since this need is about soul-searching, it induces an employee to realize his full potential for continued self-development and to seek challenging work assignments, that allow for creativity and opportunities for personal growth and advancement.

2. **ERG Theory:** This theory speculates that there are three core needs of every individual. They are existence, relatedness and growth. Maslow's Need Hierarchy Theory is further expanded by Alderfer who termed his theory as ERG.

   a) **Existence:** It is related to our basic needs required for our existence/survival (physiological and safety needs in hierarchy theory)

   b) **Relatedness:** It is concerned with an individual's aspiration to maintain healthy interpersonal relationships. (Social Needs in Maslow's theory)

c) **Growth:** It is associated with individuals' need for personal augmentation and development. (Esteem and Self-actualization Need in Hierarchy Theory).

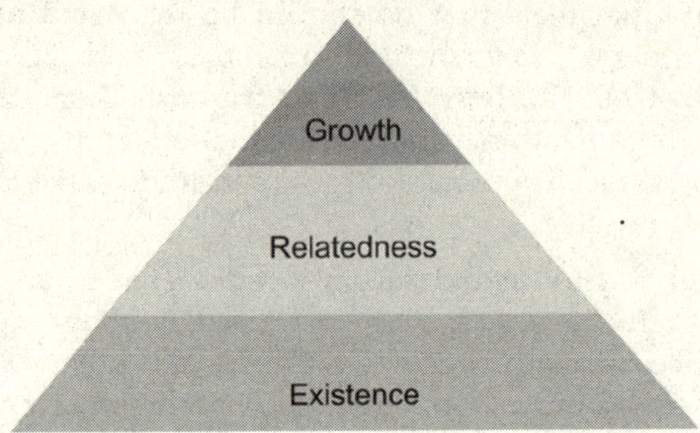

3. **Participation Theory (Theory X and Theory Y):** In this theory Maslow treated traditional approach of managing people as "Theory X" and the modern/professional approach to management as "Theory Y".

➢ Douglas McGregor (1906-1964) was an eminent American psychologist and leading contributor to organizational theory from human relations perspective. In 1960, he first presented his idea on "Theory X and Theory Y" in his famous book "*The human side of enterprise*". He formulated two sets of assumptions about human behaviour: -

➢ **Theory X:**

a. It assumes people are not creative.

b. They are dull and lazy.

c. They lack rational thinking.

d. They dislike work, work as less as possible and will avoid it if they can.

e. They are not ambitious.

f. They are irresponsible and will always try to transfer their responsibilities to others.

g. Average people prefer to be followed. They constantly seek guidance and direction from others.

h. People lack creativity, since they are orthodox in nature and resist new ideas.

i. They do not use their intellectual potentials and are unable to take advantage of the opportunities that come in their way.

j. They are self-centered, lack self-motivation and work for their personal interest only.

- **Theory Y:**

a. It assumes people are creative.

b. They accept responsibility for their work.

c. People are active and vigilant.

d. They prefer challenging and difficult task.

e. They are self-motivated, want job autonomy, can work with limited leadership and guidance.

f. They are ambitious.

g. They exercise self-control, self-direction and work in the interest of the organization.

h. People think rationally and use their creativity in solving organizational problems.

4. **Two Factor Theory of Motivation:** This theory discussed hygiene/ maintenance factors such as salary, job security, work conditions, organizational policies, mission, vision, values, and motivational factors such as achievement, recognition growth opportunities, challenging task as the prime motivational factors.

Fredrick Herzberg, an American psychologist, in the late 1950's, proposed an influential "two-factor theory" of motivation. Herzberg developed his theory after surveying 200 accountants, engineers and other managerial personnel's in nine different companies in Pittsburgh, USA.

The information collected was related to the attitude of people towards work. He asked them when they felt good or bad about their jobs. Their replies helped him to categorise various needs of individuals into two groups:

Bad feeling were job dissatisfiers and hence termed as "hygiene factors or maintenance factors" whereas good feelings were job satisfiers and hence "motivation factors".

i. **Hygiene factors:** These factors do not motivate employees, however, if they are absent, dissatisfaction can occur, hence are called "dissatisfiers" because they only prevent dissatisfaction. Such factors are:

   - Money and compensation
   - Status
   - Personal life
   - Working conditions
   - Company policies and administration
   - Supervision
   - Working relations
   - Job security
   - Welfare facilities.

ii. **Motivation factors:** Job motivation factors (also called as satisfiers) make employee happy, positive, loyal, and dedicated to the organization because they serve man's basic needs for psychological growth. It includes:

   - Challenging task
   - Added responsibility
   - Appreciation and recognition
   - Personal growth
   - Delegation of authority
   - Career development
   - Challenging task
   - Achievement of desired objectives.

For any employee these factors heavily contribute as a positive impact on the ability and efficiency of work.

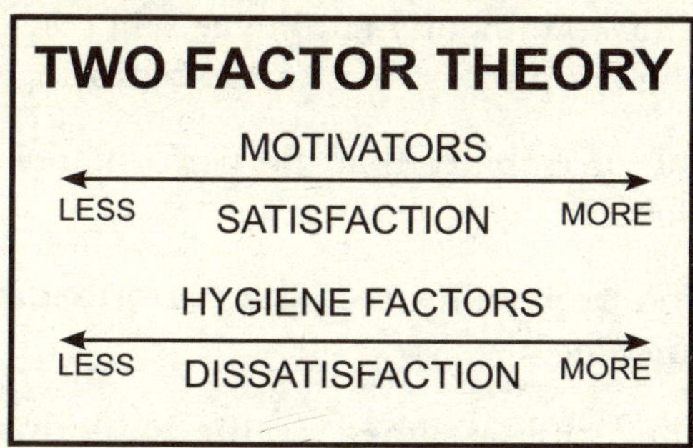

5. **Three Needs Theory:** This theory talks about three important needs. Need for achievement, power, and affiliation. David McClelland's Three Need model is related to Herzberg's motivation-hygiene theory. His model is mainly concerned with three motives:

   a) **Need for achievement:** Employees with high need for achievements are self-motivated, self-controlled and goal oriented. They accept responsibility and demonstrate their skills and abilities.

   b) **Need for affiliation:** Employees with high need for affiliation values interpersonal relationships. They are more concerned toward's other employees.

   c) **Need for power:** Employees with high need for power seek to dictate command or have control over people.

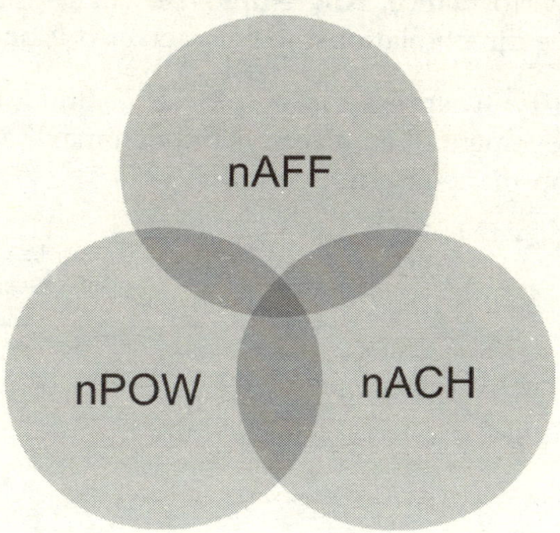

6. **Expectancy Theory:** This theory which explains valence, instrumentality and expectancy as the major motivational factors. Valence-expectancy theory was originally proposed by Victor H.

Vroom. According to him, any employee will consider the following three elements before putting an effort to perform a task.

a) What is the probability that the performance will be up to the expected level?

b) What is the probability that the performance will lead to the desired outcome?

c) What is the value assigned by the individual to the potential outcome? He explained that an individual's motivation level would be determined by his perception that a certain type of action would lead to a specific outcome. Vroom suggested the relationship between three variables which have a high positive impact on the individual's performance but also demonstrates that if any one of the variable is zero, then the total motivation also results in zero. Their relationship is explained in the following formula:

Motivation = Valence *Expectancy* Instrumentality

Valence: It refers to an individual's preference for a reward on the achievement of a specific outcome, i.e., how much reward one wants on achievement/ attainment of desired result.

Expectancy: It is a probability that a particular action will lead to a desired reward/performance. Any employee will be motivated to work only when they see direct relationship between efforts and rewards.

Instrumentality: It expresses an employee's estimate that performance will result in achievement of an objective or outcome. It can be in the form of monetary or non-monetary motivation.

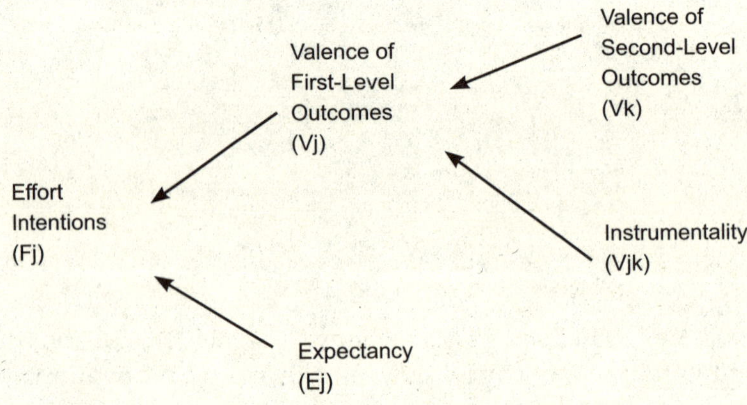

7. **The Porter - Lawler Model:** It is based on the assumption that motivation does not always lead to satisfaction or performance.

This model was suggested by Lyman W. Porter and Edward E. Lawler III. It is an expansion of the expectancy theory model proposed by Victor H. Vroom. According to Porter and Lawler through appropriate rewards, performance can be enhanced and better performance can lead to satisfaction. Thus there is a need to carefully study the efforts-performance-reward-satisfaction structure. This can be better explained with the help of the following diagram:

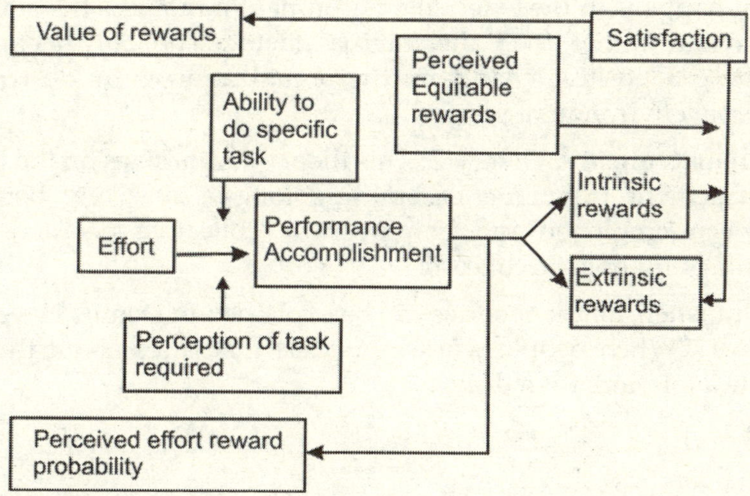

8. **Equity Theory:** This theory discusses that employee wants firm and fair treatment at their work-place.

   - This theory was developed by J. Stancy Adams. It refers to the subjective judgment of an employee related to his job inputs (like educational qualifications, skills, experience, expertise, efforts, etc,) in comparison with the outcome (which includes salary, bonus, incentives, allowances and other non-monetary rewards).
   - If an employee feels that his inputs are more than the output, he may get dissatisfied, this can effect the quality, quantity, productivity or efficiency of the employee (in worst case he may even resign from his job).
   - If rewards are more than the inputs they may work harder.
   - If they are proportionally rewarded (output=input) then they will continue with their efforts and maintain their productivity and efficiency level.

9. **B.K Shiner's Reinforcement Theory:** This theory analyzed that what happens in the external environment influences the employee's behaviour rather than the internal factor. The only technique of creating a positive change in the organization is by designing the external environment properly.
10. **William Ounchi's Theory Z:** This theory emphasizes on the Japanese management technique of building long-term strong bond, trust between employee and employer by collective decision-making, training and holistic concern.

In a nutshell, all the theories can be explained in Dennis Hayes words which says, "When people work in a place that cares about them, they contribute a lot more than duty".

Types of Motivation

In an organization some employees are internally motivated, while some depend on external motivation. Inner motivation is the talent and capability to indulge oneself emotionally and physically to achieve the desired target/ goal, by overcoming problems and hurdles.

> ***"The turning point, I think, was when I realized that you can do it yourself. That you have to believe in you because sometime that's the only person that does believe in your success but you"***
>
> *—Tim Blixseth*

Internally motivated personalities are people who:

- Have a sound and rational decision-making approach.
- In stressful situations, are usually calm, cool, composed, and confident.
- Trust their knowledge, skills and ability.
- Focus on their strengths.
- Have a self-determined priority towards work.
- Measure their own performance and compare them with set standards.
- Don't require external rewards or treats to perform their task.
- Force themselves beyond any determined boundaries, limits, restrictions and limitations through their will-power, team work, devotion, dedication, loyalty and commitment.
- Do not depend on external forces to motivate or demotivate them.
- Believe, "success or failure all depend on us". The more we are motivated the greater will be the desire to achieve our target.
- Are self-disciplined, organized and have a long-term action plan. To achieve their long-term goals they maintain a "to-do-list".

- Follow their own instinct, perception and hunch.
- Accept change as a part of life.
- Are balanced, confident, responsive, enthusiastic and composed.

Externally motivated employees expect gratification from others. As Tony Dorsett rightly feels that, to succeed, you need to find something to hold on to, something to motivate you, something to inspire you. External motivation can be in the form of monetary and non-monetary rewards.

Monetary forces are attractive salary/wages, bonus, incentives, commission, allowances, employee stock option, merit-pay, pay-for-performance, profit/gain sharing to enhance the performance of the employee. As Takafumi Horie rightly says, "Money is human kind's greatest invention. Money doesn't care whether a person comes from a good family, or what his skin color is. Anybody can make money".

Whereas, growth opportunity and development, recognition of good work, participation in key decision making, autonomy, flexible working hours, a pat on the back, a letter of appreciation, decent treatment, job security, hygienic work environment are the few non-monetary motivational factors at work-place.

"I can live for two months on a good compliment"

—Mark Twain

Some researchers have identified a direct relationship between monetary rewards and work performance. Hence, an organization needs a balance financial and non-financial motivation to maximize the job performance. As the saying goes, motivation is the art of getting people to do what you want them to do as if they want to do it.

An internally motivated employee knows the art of stress management. So what is stress? Can it be managed? If yes, then how?

Things Work Out

Because it rains when we wish it wouldn't,
Because men do what they often shouldn't,
Because crops fail, and plans go wrong
Some of us grumble all day long.
But somehow, in spite of the care and doubt,
It seems at last that things work out.
Because we lose where we hoped to gain,
Because we suffer a little pain,
Because we must work when we'd like to play

Some of us whimper along life's way.
But somehow, as day always follows the night,
Most of our troubles work out all right.
Because we cannot forever smile,
Because we must trudge in the dust awhile,
Because we think that the way is long
Some of us whimper that life's all wrong.
But somehow we live and our sky grows bright,
And everything seems to work out all right.
So bend to your trouble and meet your care,
For the clouds must break, and the sky grow fair.
Let the rain come down, as it must and will,
But keep on working and hoping still.
For in spite of the grumblers who stand about,
Somehow, it seems, all things work out.

—Edgar A. Guest

Stress Management at Workplace

At the workplace, we all face certain amount of stress in the form of deadlines, competition, saturation, pressure, sorrow, etc., the causes of which can be job insecurity, high demand for performance (unrealistic expectations), expansion of technology, personal or family problems resulting in typical symptoms of job stress such as loss of mental concentration, anxiety, absenteeism, depression and heart/stomach/back problems.

Hans Selye was one of the founding fathers of research on stress. In 1956 he was of the opinion that, "Stress is not necessarily something bad – it all depends on how you take it. Stress is exhilarating, creative successful work is beneficial, while that of failure, humiliation or infection is detrimental". Our goal, however, shouldn't be to eliminate stress but to learn how to manage stress and how to use it to help us. Positive stress adds to anticipation and excitement. Fortunately, stress management is largely a learnable skill.

10 Long-term Survival Mantras

1. **Develop positive attitude towards stressful situations in life:**

   As said: If we think happy thoughts, we will be happy

   If we think miserable thoughts, we will be miserable

   If we think fearful thoughts, we will be fearful,

   Happiness is harvest, stress is weeds.

   Each one of us cannot be great and do great things; we can do small things greatly and become stress free. What is important is developing a positive attitude even when forced with challenging situations.

2. **Laughter is the best medicine:** Laughter lowers the blood pressure and reduces hypertension. "Laugh and even the birds laugh with you, laughter is like a prayer. If you can laugh, you have learnt how to pray.

Don't be serious. Only a person who can laugh not only at others, but at himself also, can be religious." —Osho Rajneesh. It helps to kill stress. For every 10 minutes you are stressed, you lose 600 seconds of happiness.

3. **Inculcate the habit of "forgive and forget":** As Martin Luther King rightly said, "Forgiveness is not an occasional act, it is a permanent attitude." The relationship between the two is that: Forgiving allows another person to forgive another for faults, mistakes, or misdeeds. Forgetting puts these griviences behind. They are no longer brought up and not allowed to be a barrier to your relationship. Try to change yourself before you change others because you cannot change everyone.

4. **Always be kind and gentle with yourself:** Be your best friend. Start work early, get adequate rest to maintain your energy level. Occasionally, pamper yourself with a treat, weekend offs, trying out new food and shopping. Keep a check on your weight. Excess weight increases the stress on our body, making it more prone to certain chronic diseases such as high blood pressure, diabetes and cardiac disorder.

5. **Smoking induces stress:** Although adult smokers state that smoking helps them, a research conducted shows that, contrary to their belief, it actually heightens tension, irritability, depression. Smokers are actually more stressed than non-smokers. In addition, the other consequences of smoking can be skin problem (skin rashes), bad breath, smelly clothes, reduced athletic performance, greater risk of injuries and increased time for healing.

6. **Practice yogic techniques for stress relief:** The benefits of yoga postures (Asana), breathing (Pranayama), and meditation (Dhyana) awareness in our bodies releases muscular tension and enhances coordination between mind and body, thus ensuring an overall feeling of well-being. Sit straight and comfortably on your seat and try the deep breathing exercise. Breathe deeply. As the air flows, don't try to control your breath. This type of breathing relaxes the body, mind and relieves you of stress.

7. **Utilize time preciously and usefully:** Set your goals to conquer stress. Maintain a "to-do-list" and a "planner" to avoid postponements. Start now what has to be done later and you will soon reach the final line. Let me tell you the story of four People named Everybody, Somebody, Anybody and Nobody. There was an important job to be done and Everybody was sure that Somebody would do it. Anybody could

have done it but Nobody did it. Somebody got angry about that because it was Everybody's job. Everybody thought Anybody could do it but Nobody realized that Everybody wouldn't do it. It ended up that Everybody blamed Somebody when Nobody did what Anybody could have done.

8. **Develop the self-confidence you deserve:** Jack Welch feels, "Confidence gives you courage and extends your reach. It lets you take greater risks and achieve far more than you ever thought possible". This powerfully conveys the enormous role that self-confidence plays in reducing stress and achieving success. Never take criticism personally.

9. **Identify burn-out:** Burn-out reduces productivity and also saps your energy. Take small breaks during long spells of work and engage your mind off stress by developing some kind of hobbies, speak to old friends, surf the Internet, listen to music, etc.

10. **Learn to love your work:** Be proud of what you do for a living. Never lose respect, because he, who cannot respect his work, cannot expect others to respect him. Always remember: if you become the chairman of company, what purpose will it serve if, in the process, you get divorced and your children get addicted to drugs. Hence, maintain a healthy work-life balance.

My Creed

To live as gently as I can; To be, no matter where, a man;
To take what comes of good or ill, And cling to faith and honor still;
To do my best, and let that stand the record of my brain and hand;
And then, should failure come to me, Still work and hope for victory.
To have no secret place wherein; I stoop unseen to shame or sin;
To be the same when I'm alone; As when my every deed is known.
To live undaunted, unafraid of any step that I have made;
To be without pretense or shame; Exactly what men think I am.
To leave some simple mark behind; To keep my having lived in mind,
If enmity to aught I show, To be an honest, generous foe,
To play my little part, nor whine; That greater honours are not mine.
This, I believe, is all I need for my philosophy and creed.

—Edgar A. Guest

17 Monetary and Non-Monetary Rewards

Monetary and non-monetary motivation can be positive or negative. This is further explained in the following table:

Table 1: Monetary and non-monetary motivation techniques.

	POSITIVE	**NEGATIVE**
Monetary	Salary Bonus Incentives ESOP Allowances Commission	Reduction in salary Demotion No bonus/ incentives
Non-Monetary	Appreciation Delegation Encouragement Recognition Praise Employee Participation	Punishment Criticism Fear of loss of job Indecent treatment Unhygienic environment

Clarence Francis, the former Chairman of General Foods (USA), once said, "You can buy a man's time; you can buy a man's physical presence at a given place.... but you cannot buy his initiative, you cannot buy loyalty.... you have to earn these things." Detailed description of various methods are discussed in the later chapters. Here's a brief overview of the various monetary and non-monetary motivation.

Monetary Motivation

1. **Salary and wages:** Various researches have revealed that money is the most important motivating factors for the employees. Salary must be paid on time and should be revised occasionally.

2. **Bonus:** Under the Bonus Payment Act, 1965 a listed company has to declare bonus whenever it earns profit. It is an additional payment given to employees normally once a year which increases their income and motivates them to perform better.

3. **Incentives:** It is an additional payment, over and above their salaries for their additional efforts and contribution. It is to reward and recognize better performance of some of the employees as compared to others.

4. **Allowance:** The management may also provide additional benefits such as, medical allowance, leave, travel allowance, overtime allowance, dearness allowance, conveyance allowance, etc, which acts as positive motivators.

5. **Exceptional incentives:** Such incentives are offered only to certain deserving employees for their valuable idea, thoughts, analysis, judgment, annotations, etc. Such monetary incentives include performance bonus, attendance bonus, etc.

6. **Merit pay:** In this catagory every individual employee reward is proportional to performance. By implementing merit pay (also known as pay for performance) organization is directly rewarding high performers to boost their morale and sends an indicator to the remaining employees that they must try to overcome their weaknesses in future to perform better.

7. **ESOP:** Employee stock option plan gives an opportunity to the employees to purchase their company's share at a future date, at a given price. It is an important performance incentive because employees have ownership share in the organization and motivates them to work hard to raise the share price which in return provides monetary gain to the employees.

8. **Pension plan:** Organizations offer various types of retirement benefits to their employees once they retire.

Non-Monetary Motivation

1. **Job security:** Employees who are hired on temporary/probation basis often feel disappointed because they feel that they can be thrown out from the organization anytime. Thus job guarantee keep the employee away from any stress of this kind.

2. **Status:** Employees are often seen to be very proud of their fancy designations, hence when employees are provided with better job titles it enhances their position and gives them a feel good factor.

3. **Appreciation:** Appreciating good work and publically recognizing their efforts with suitable awards, rewards and prizes, act as a good motivator for employers.

4. **Delegation of authority:** Authority will always flow in a downward direction, i.e., from top to bottom. With proper delegation of authority (given to fulfill certain responsibility) employees feel that their superiors have trust in them and thus take more interest and initiative to meet their boss's expectations.

5. **Work conditions:** The work environment should be enjoyable, safe and convincingly comfortable. It includes proper fans, lighting, ventilation, sanitation, layout, machines, tools, techniques, equipment, recreation, canteen, etc. thus, a congenial work environment is important for employee motivation.

6. **Job enrichment:** It provides an opportunity to employees for greater positive reception, encroachment by providing more challenging work and additional responsibilities which gives them an opportunity to explore their creativity, be an innovator and even an inventor.

7. **Labour participation:** By encouraging employees to share their valuable thoughts, analysis and encouraging criticisms, advices, comments, proposals, interpretations, the management can build a healthy two-way communication with the employees. This way they can express their thoughts easily and feel a part of the organization. The management can also suitably reward few healthy comments to encourage their employees.

8. **Career development opportunities:** Such as encouraging employees to constantly update and upgrade their knowledge through proper training and development; fair promotion, transfer and growth opportunities; fair treatment to all the workers irrespective of their gender, age, status, caste, religion, nationality, etc., also motivate employees and help develop thier personalities as well.

9. **Flexible hours:** Occasionally allowing employees to come late or leave early to meet some of their personal obligations can help increase their impetus.

Napoleon Bonaparte once said, "Give me enough medals and I'll win you any war". Employees can be extremely efficient, useful, and successful, when they are positively motivated. Positive motivation instills high self-esteem, spirit and confidence and promotes team spirit. It inspires and stimulates employees to perform better.

In general, positive motivation is acceptable, as someone rightly said, "what gets recognized gets done and get rewarded gets repeated".

Some researchers argue that intrinsic motivation doesn't exist, some say that employees perform better when they do something only because they get rewarded or threatened to perform. A research conducted by American Society for Training and Development (ASTD) revealed that consistent employee recognition is the core factor in retaining employees.

Thus, to understand the impact of both Positive (Monetary/ Non-Monetary) and Negative (Monetary/Non-Monetary) motivation for enhancing job performance, the author conducted a survey of 25 employees. The survey revealed that:

- 45% employees believed that internal motivation is the best form of motivation, whereas 35% believed that external motivation is needed. The rest believed that both are needed to produce maximum result.
- When asked why an employee needs motivation, about 60% workers said that it serves to increase their efficiency and effectiveness, which further helps to boost their productivity and performance, while 40% required motivation for their personal development and growth of the organization.
- In contrary to the popular belief, when asked to prioritize their highest motivational factor, 12% emphasized on bonus/ incentives; 11% opted for recognition, participation in decision-making, pay-for-performance and growth opportunity, whereas 9% wanted employee stock option scheme, flexible work hours, autonomy/independence, 6% required gain/profit sharing, and finally, only 5% asked for medals, awards and certificates.
- In addition to the above mentioned motivational factors, some said that an employee needs a congenial work environment having friendly employer-employee relationship, and occasional informal gatherings like annual picnic/sports/entertainment events etc. for motivation towards work.

Thus, motivation is the inner drive to perform a task effectively and produce best results both qualitatively and quantitatively. It is the desire to achieve the determined goal. Employees at all levels need continuous motivation, although the tools to motivate them may vary.

Finally, it can be concluded by referring to Vince Lombardi's statement that says that a man can be as great as he wants and have the courage, determination, dedication, the competitive drive and if you are willing to sacrifice little things in life and pay the price for the things that are worthwhile, it can be done.

50 Motivational Quotes that Inspire

Here, are a few motivational quotes that never fail to inspire us:

1. ***The only way of finding the limits of the possible is by going beyond them into the impossible.***

   —Arthur C. Clarke

2. ***If you do not hope, you will not find what is beyond your hopes.***

   —St. Clement of Alexandra

3. ***Don't wait to strike till the iron is hot; but make it hot by striking.***

   —William B. Sprague

4. ***The more difficulties one has to encounter, within and without, the more significant and the higher in inspiration his life will be.***

   —Horace Bushnell

5. ***Without inspirations, the best powers of the mind remain dormant; they are a fuel in us which needs to be ignited with sparks.***

   —Johann Gottfried Von Herder

6. ***Along with success comes a reputation for wisdom.***

   —Euripides

7. ***Courage is like love; it must have hope for nourishment.***

   —Napoleon

8. ***Nothing can stop the man with the right mental attitude from achieving his goal; nothing on earth can help the man with the wrong mental attitude.***

   —Thomas Jefferson

9. *The thing always happens that you really believe in; and the belief in a thing makes it happen.*

—Frank Lloyd Wright

10. *If you wish success in life make perseverance your bosom friend, experience your wise counselor, caution your elder brother and hope your guardian genius.*

—Joseph Addison

11. *Circumstances! Make circumstances.*

—Napoleon

12. *Don't limit yourself; many people limit themselves to what they think they can do. You can go as far as your mind lets you. What you believe, remember you can achieve.*

—Mary Kay Ash

13. *If you are not willing to risk the unusual, you will have to settle for the ordinary.*

—Jim Rohn

14. *Whatever the mind of man can conceive and believe it can achieve. Thoughts are things! And powerful things at that, when mixed definiteness of purpose, and burning desire, can be translated into riches.*

—Napoleon Hill

15. *Live out of your imagination, not your history*

— Stephen Covey

16. *We will either find a way, or make one.*

—Hannibal

17. *The miracle is not to fly in the air, or to walk on the water; but to walk on the earth.*

—Chinese Proverb

18. *You are never too old to set another goal or to dream a new dream.*

—Les Brown

19. *We must risk going too far to discover just how far we can go.*

—Jim Rohn

20. *The enemy of the "best" is the "good"*

21. *If an egg is broken by an outside force...a life ends.*
If an egg breaks from within....Life begins. (Great things always begin from within).

—Jay McLean

22. *It's better to lose your ego to the one you love. Than to lose the one you love.... Because of ego.*

—John Keats

23. *Never stop. One stops as soon as something is about to happen.*

—Peter Brock

24. *Why we have so many temples, if god is everywhere? A wise man said: air is everywhere, but we still need a fan to feel it.*

—Anonymous

25. *When you trust someone trust him completely without any doubt... At the end you would get one of the two: either a lesson for your life or a very good person.*

—Umesh Natraj

26. *You've got to get up every morning with determination if you're going to go to bed with satisfaction.*

—George Lorimar

27. *Life is not about the people who act true to your face. It's about the people who remain true behind your back.*

28. *Soldier: sir we are surrounded from all sides by enemies, Major: excellent! We can attack in any direction.*

29. *Do not follow where the path may lead. Go instead where is no path and leave a trail.*

—Harold R. McAlindon

30. *The worst in life is "attachment" it hurts when you lose it. The best thing in life is "loneliness" because it teaches you everything and, when you lose it, you get everything.*

31. *You never conquer a mountain. You stand on the summit a few moments; then the wind blows your footprints away.*

—Arlene Blum

32. *The greatest waste in the world is the difference between what we are and what we could become.*

—Ben Herbste

33. *Prayer is not a "spare wheel" that you pull out when in trouble, but it is a "steering wheel" that directs the right path throughout.*

34. *The future depends on what we do in the present.*

—Mahatma Gandhi

35. *Knowing is not enough; we must apply. Willing is not enough; we must do.*

—Johann Wolfgang von Goethe

36. *No great man ever complains of want of opportunities.*

—Ralph Waldo Emerson

37. *We are all inventors, each sailing out on a voyage of discovery, guided each by a private chart, of which there is no duplicate. The world is all gates, all opportunities.*

—Ralph Waldo Emerson

38. *So a car's windshield is so large and the rear view mirror is so small? Because our past is not as important as our future. So, Look Ahead and Move on.*

—Billy Cox

39. *A failure is a man who has blundered, but is not able to cash in on the experience.*

—Elbert Hubbard

40. *Friendship is like a book. It takes few seconds to burn, but it takes years to write.*

—Fr Charbel Habchi

41. *All things in life are temporary. If going well, enjoy it, they will not last forever. If going wrong, don't worry, they can't last long either.*

42. *Old Friends are Gold! New Friends are Diamond! If you get a Diamond, don't forget the Gold! Because to hold a Diamond, you always need a Base of Gold!*

43. *Often when we lose hope and think this is the end, God smiles from above and says, "Relax, sweetheart, it's just a bend, not the end!*

44. *When God solves your problems, you have faith in His abilities; when God doesn't solve your problems He has faith in your abilities.*

45. *A blind person asked St. Anthony: "Can there be anything worse than losing eye sight?" He replied: "Yes, losing your vision!"*

46. *When you pray for others, God listens to you and blesses them, and sometimes, when you are safe and happy, remember that someone has prayed for you.*
47. *Worrying does not take away tomorrow's troubles; it takes away today's peace.*
48. *God didn't have time to make a nobody, only a somebody. I believe that each of us has God-given talents within us waiting to be brought to fruition.*

    —Mary Kay Ash

49. *There is only one success — to be able to spend your life in your own way.*

    —Christopher Morley

50. *The secret of success is to know something nobody else knows.*

    —Aristotle Onassis

The Challenge

Let others lead small lives,
But not you.
Let others argue over small things,
But not you.
Let others cry over small hurts,
But not you.
Let others leave their future
In someone else's hands,
But not you.

—Jim Rohn

Work Environment and Employee Motivation

Research has shown that there exists a relationship between a "congenial work environment" and "employee motivation". An enthusiastic spirit in the work environment replenishes the liveliness of the organization and converts it into quality output. Such is the impact that is visible in an employee's performance, approach, productivity, efficiency, performance and that overall behaviour. Negativity often results in loss of self-assurance, self-confidence, self-belief, self-reliance, self-control and mental stability.

There are various factors such as autonomy, remuneration standards, work pressure superior-subordinate relationship, career development opportunities, organizational vision, encouragement to creativity, appreciation by seniors, good leaders, job stability/security, firm and fair organizational policies, trust, flexibility, team spirit, etc, that contributes to workplace motivation.

Thus, a positive work environment is important irrespective of the size/nature and type of business organization. Creating such environment is the task of the employer, since such environment benefits not only in the employees, but also the employer, has a domino effect in the form of reduced turnover/wastages/interruption in work/damages/disruption and promotes allegiance, devotion, fidelity and dependability on each other. In an affirmative work environment, average performers' productivity also increases whereas, the reverse is also true.

Continuous employee motivation is challenging yet a priority for all employers because employee motivation has a direct impact on their jobs. Unenthusiastic employees drain their time and energy in unproductive chores and constantly criticize their subordinates/superiors/assignments/organization/external factors, etc.

They persistently spread rumours, chit-chat, indulge in inter group/intra group conflicts and are always sad, disheartened, discontent, unhappy and regret their decisions of working with the organization. There are number of books addressing this issue. Some of the renowned authors are Jim Collins, *"Why some companies make a leap... And other's don't"*, *Gary S. Topchik, "Managing Workplace Negativity"*, *Ferdinand Fornies, "Why Employees don't do what they're supposed to do and what to do about it"*.

There are certain secret codes, symbols and languages to identify a pessimist work environment like:

- Constant critic from employees regarding the company's plans, policies, functioning, approach of seniors/management, etc.
- High employee attrition rate
- Frequent abseentism
- Low team spirit
- Negative response/comments on change management
- Lack of interest
- Pessimistic attitude
- Distrust/back stabbing, etc.

However; here are a few simple strategies to overcome these problems and create a favourable work environment:

a. To create an ideal work environment, identify the reasons for lack of enthusiasm/unconstructiveness/pessimist behaviour of the employee (reasons can be many and are stated in the following chapters). It is beneficial to take suitable actions in the inception stage itself and pay attention to the early warning signs. For identifying the reasons for their insecurity and apprehensiveness, ask yourself questions such as:

   What is the problem?

   Why has this problem occurred?

   Since **When** is it existing?

   Where can we look for solutions?

   Who will be an influencing element to overcome this problem?

   How can this problem be overcome?

The answers to these questions will provide a clear picture about the problem and also suggest various remedies to overcome the problem. As aptly said by **William Arthur Ward**, "Do more than belong: participate. Do more than care: help. Do more than believe: practice. Do more than be fair: be kind. Do more than forgive: forget. Do more than dream: work".

b. Give employees suitable authority, power and command.

c. Ask employees to share their valuable suggestions, opinions, outlook about company's plans, policies, goals and strategies. Since taking constant feedback of the employees will help you in identifying the symptoms of the lack of enthusiasm at the work-place and lack of zeal and zest.

d. Treat people with evenhandedness and uniformly.

e. Develop a two-way effective communication channel.

f. Foster team spirit and fortitude of each and every employee.

g. Give monetary and non-monetary remunerations since employees like acknowledgement for their work.

h. Clearly communicate the rules, regulations, vision, mission, goals, policies, plans and procedures to all employees to overcome duplication of task and disappointment.

i. Striking a clear balance between organizational objectives and employees motivation is crucial.

j. Convey your expectations and anticipations in advance. Nevertheless, also mention the usual performance standards for the employees based on their job specification.

k. Make a conscious effort to constantly overcome hurdles, obstacles and difficulties.

l. Use simple and powerful motivational tools to exhibit concern.

m. To break their monotony, promote testing, trailing and experimentation (which definitely involves calculated risk).

n. Try to eliminate non-value adding activities to reduce wastages.

o. Encourage amity, companionship and comradeship among employees.

42 Reasons Why Employees Lack Motivation?

Employees who lack motivation are usually passive, inactive, careless, less considerate and unkind. They prefer playing the blame game and have many excuses to hide their incompetency. Very often, they are unhappy and dissatisfied.

There can be several reasons why employees lack motivation.

- Lack of conviction
- Low self-confidence
- Fear of rejection
- Unable to accept change
- Lack of time
- Office politics
- Lack of professionalism
- Monotony
- Stress/burnout
- No rewards/incentives
- Unsupportive superiors
- Unrealistic expectations
- Little sense of accomplishment of task
- Lack of career direction
- Limited training facilities
- Lack of career development opportunities

- Lack of feedback
- Lack of interest in final outcomes
- Feeling of isolation
- No work empowerment
- Rigid work schedule
- Severe punishments
- Lack of skills and capabilities
- Avoidance of work
- Being passive
- Feelings misunderstood
- Fear of failure
- Past failures
- Lack of self-respect
- Unfavourable external environment
- Disinterest/boredom
- Delay in decision-making
- Ignorance
- Sluggishness
- Lack of priorities
- Lack of knowledge
- Lack of vision
- Lack of assertiveness
- Domestic problems
- Negative self-talk
- Constant comparison with others
- Criticism, etc.

Life

They told me that Life could be just what I made it
Life could be fashioned and worn like a gown;
I, the designer, mine the decision
Whether to wear it with bonnet or crown.
And so I selected the prettiest pattern
Life should be made of the rosiest hue
Something unique, and a bit out of fashion,
One that perhaps would be chosen by few.
But other folks came and they leaned o'er my shoulder;
Someone questioned the ultimate cost;
Somebody tangled the thread I was using;
One day I found that my scissors were lost.
And somebody claimed the material faded;
Somebody said I'd be tired ere 'twas worn;
Somebody's fingers, too pointed and spiteful,
Snatched at the cloth, and I saw it was torn.

—Nan Terrell Reed

What is Inner Motivation?

The man who makes a success of an important venture never wails for the crowd. He strives out for himself. It takes nerves, it takes a great lot of grit, but the man that succeeds has both. Anyone can fail. The public admires the man who has enough confidence in himself to take a chance. These chances are the main things after all. The man who tries to succeed must expect to be criticized.

> ***"Nothing important was ever done but the greater number consulted previously doubted the possibility. Success is the accomplishment of that which most people think can't be done"***
>
> *—C. V. White*

We often wonder at some of the business tycoons such as J.R.D Tata, Dhirubhai Ambani, Azim Premji, and Narayan Murthy who inspite of all the challenges during their career, converted those stumbling blocks into stepping stones of success. The driving factor for them was their **inner strength and internal motivation** that pushed them to overcome every hurdle beyond any perceived limit or boundary. They firmly believed that if we doubt ourselves we can never achieve anything great.

If we have the necessary confidence, ability, and knowledge, then positive outcome will definitely follow up. They desperatly wanted to win and a determined person can easily figure out how to make things happen. They believe that the difference between success and failure lies in their self-determination and internal motivation.

They may have agreed with Lloyd Wright, when he said that the thing always happens that one really believed in, and the belief makes it happen.

Recently I read a small story on positive thinking. Here it goes...

It was a hot summer day, a man was travelling to a far of place. Having walked for hours he got really tired and hungry. He saw a big Banyan tree and was happy to rest under the shade. While he was resting and enjoying the cool breeze, he thought: I wish I had some delicious food to eat. Soon, a lady came by and offered some food to him. He really enjoyed the meal and ate to his satisfaction. He thanked the lady and was lying down on the hard surface. When he thought: I wish I had a nice thick mat to sleep on. Seeing him lying on the ground, the same lady who fed him felt sad to see him sleeping on the hard surface, went home and brought a mat for him. So he was very happy and tried to get some sleep. His legs were tired and he thought: I wish I had somebody to massage my tired legs. Then the same lady sensed his need and sent her daughter to massage his tired legs. She went home after some time. Then he thought: I am lying down not very far from the forest. What if a tiger comes and attacks me during my sleep! Exactly what happened. A tiger came, attacked him and killed him."[1]

This seems like a silly story, but conveys a great message:

"What we focus on, we empower and enlarge. Good multiplies when focused upon. Negativity multiplies when focused upon. The choice is ours: What do we want more of?"

In an article published by Iswariya Viswa Vidyaalaya, it spoke of three important advises. They are:

1. The quality of thoughts decides the quality of outcomes .
2. Thoughts have the power to find expression because they are instrumental in channeling energy towards the physical or mental condition.
3. External situations and remarks can harm us through our thoughts - but only to the extent our thoughts allow them to. So the key is to think positive.

In my interactions with different .people across the country, one common question has always stood out. In any organization, why do some people repeatedly achieve their goals while some struggle to achieve even a single objective?

The answer lies with the individuals. Ability to inspire and motivate himself from within, his capability to analyze who and what motivates him to move forward. His belief that inner motivation will drive towards desire, discipline and direction which help him to achieve his target.

The advantages of internally motivated employees are:

- They see the doughnut, not the hole.
- They follow their intuition and gut feeling.

---

[1]Source: www.indiadivine.org

- They are firm, focused and passionate.
- They always recognize opportunity as they find grass greener on their side.
- They stay away from employees who have negative attitude; because they believe that a worker is influenced not only by positive thinkers but also by negative company.
- They compete against themselves and critically identify the factors that are holding them back.
- They are content with their job – yet ambitious.
- They accept failure, learn from them and never repeat them.
- They inspire loyalty, team-spirit within the department and the organization.
- They enjoy every stage and phase of work.
- Their performance shoots up in testing times.
- They know inner motivation is limitless, infinite, contagious, unrestrictive, unconstrained, unrestrained and indefinite.
- They know when to Say No!
- They believe that life is an echo; you get back what you give.
- They accept the fact that inner motivation gives them the courage to imagine beyond what they think is possible and achievable.
- They are dedicated, committed and devoted.
- They always speak the truth.
- They maintain a congenial relationship with others.
- They never stress themselves too much since continuous failures may reduce their self-confidence.
- They are trained to bring solutions/answers for their problems or difficulties.
- Overall, they encourage an environment that is encouraging, stimulating, and inspiring.

There is a direct relationship between the way we feel about ourselves and our attitude. If we feel great from within, we develop a positive attitude and our productivity improves. The reverse is also true. Without inner motivation, an employee easily becomes disinterested in work, stays tired, rigid, lethargic, bored and unconcerned. To put in simple words, he becomes an unproductive member of the organization.

Take some time off and answer the following questions:

- Do you love your job?

- Are you proud of your work?
- Does it excite you?
- Do you constantly strive to achieve bigger and better targets?
- Do you feel you are giving your 100%?

If the answer to all the above questions is yes, congratulations! You are an asset to the company. If no, then sorry, you need to inspire and encourage yourself from within. Follow Rob. E. Geraghty's suggestion that the answer, maybe, is going out and doing rather than waiting. If you wait, life will probably pass you.

However, if you go out and do things you want to, take risks, you will find that everything falls into place. You can either externally motivate yourself (in the form of monetary/non-monetary rewards) or inspire yourself from within.

Studies have time and again demonstrated the effectiveness of inner motivation on work performance and evaluated the limitation of financial and non-financial rewards. Some psychologists revealed that external motivation is not directly related to personal satisfaction and happiness i.e., the result of peripheral compensation on productivity and efficiency may or may not always be positive. On the other hand, some researchers have pointed that employees deliver their best when they do something from within and not for some monetary/non-monetary reward.

Internally motivated employees are unprejudiced, self-assured, secured, attentive, responsive, certain, considerate, compassionate and enlightened. There are times when they are stressed, disheartened and puzzled but with inner strength and self-confidence they can face every situation and overcome them. They never get disheartened by criticism or discouraged by failure.

As Michael Jordan rightly said, "Be true to the game because the game will be true to you. If you try shortcuts in the game, then the game will short cut you".

If you put in efforts, good things will automatically come. That's true about the game; and in some ways that's true about life too.

The impact of external motivation is temporary and short-lived. Externally driven employees refuse to accept change without reward. They are unfocused, uncommitted and never accept additional responsibility.

For example: Exciting work can be a motivating factor for some workers, but some prefer monotonous daily routine task.

If we want to constantly motivate ourselves from within, we need to follow the following rules:

1. ***"If it is to be, it is up to me"***

—Anonymous

Develop a positive attitude towards your work.

2. ***The talent of success is nothing more than doing what you can do well.***

—Henry W. Longfellow

Focus on your positive points by analyzing your strengths, weaknesses area of competency, specialization and focus on your domain that dwells deep within.

3. ***The enemy of the "best" is the "good"***

—Anonymous

Expect the best and give your best.

4. ***Don't wait; the time will never be "just right". Start where you stand and work with whatever tools you have at your command and better tools will be found as you go along***

—N. Hill

Count your blessings and not pains.

5. ***It is one of the strange ironies of this strange life (that) those who work the hardest, who subject themselves to the strictest discipline who give up their certain pleasurable things in order to achieve goal are the happiest people***

— Brutus Hamilton

Work really, really hard.

6. ***The greatest discovery of my generation is that human being can alter their lives by altering their attitude of mind***

—William James

Develop a positive self-esteem and self-respect.

7. ***Get over the idea that only children should spend their time in studying. Be a student so long as you still have something to learn, and this will mean all your life***

—Henry L. Doherty

Keep learning new things every day.

8. ***Success is the sum of small efforts repeated day in and day out***

—Robert Collier

Write down the factor that motivates you, and constantly apply them.

9. ***Enthusiasm is the mother of effort and without it nothing great was ever achieved***

—Ralph Waldo Emerson

Be Enthusiastic.

10. ***When work, commitment and pleasure all become one and you reach the deep well where passion lives, nothing is impossible***

—D. H. Lawrence

Associate your target with delight pleasure, satisfaction, bliss and not pain or discomfort.

11. ***To find the road of life, the best proverb of all is that which says: — "Leave no stone unturned"***

—Edward Bulwer Lytton

Don't surrender yourself completely to your fate.

12. ***Your goals are your roadmap that guides you and shows you what is possible for your life***

—Les Brown

Have a game plan, i.e. evaluate features and characteristics like:

- What are your short/long-term plans?
- When do you want to achieve them?
- How do you want to achieve them?
- What are your strengths and weaknesses?
- Why is it important?

13. ***The more difficulties one has to encounter, within and without, the more significant and the higher inspiration his life will be***

—Horace Bushnell

Understand the fact that success is not absence of failures but despite of failures.

14. ***The talent of success is nothing more than doing what you can do well***

—Henry W. Longfellow

Stay focused on what you want and what you don't.

15. ***They can because they think they can***

—Virgil

Think like a winner.

16. ***Great spirits have always encountered violent opposition from mediocre minds***

—Albert Einstein

Recognize what motivates and demotivates you. Stay away from demotivating factors.

17. ***I learned this, through by my experiment - that if one advances confidently in the direction of his dreams and endeavors to live the life which he had imagined, he will meet with success unexpected in common hours***

—Henry David Thoreau

Identified goals, clear vision and measurable targets need no monetary and non-monetary rewards.

18. ***Procrastination is the fear of success. People procrastinate because they are afraid of the success that they know will result if they move ahead now. Because success is heavy, carries a responsibility with it, it is much easier to procrastinate and live on the "Someday I'll" philosophy***

—Denis Waitley

Be time-bound, punctual and never procrastinate.

19. ***The difference between a successful person and anothers is not lack of strength, not lack of knowledge but lack in will***

—Vince Lombardi

Effectively deliver even without supervision.

20. ***Impatience never command success***

—Edwin H. Chaplin

Be responsible, patient, reliable and dependable even in tough times.

21. ***I feel that the most important requirement in success is learning to overcome failure. You must learn to tolerate it, but never accept it***

—Reggie Jackson

Never accept stoppage, letdown, and failure disappoint you.

22. ***Change is not merely necessary to life – it is life***

—Alvin Toffler

Accept changes as a part of work-life.

23. ***Failures do what is tension relieving while winners do what is goal achieving***

—Dennis Waitley

Be loyal, dedicated, honest and confident.

24. ***Fall seven times; stand up eight***

—Japanese Proverb

Set an example of sincerity, bravery and fidelity.

25. ***If you doubt you can accomplish something, then you can't accomplish it. You have to have confidence in your ability, and then be tough enough to follow through***

—Rosalyn Carter

Be optimist about the task you are involved in and its outcome.

26. ***The future belongs to those who believe in the beauty of their dreams***

—Eleanor Roosevelt

Constantly think of innovative ideas to break the old pattern.

27. ***Stand up to your obstacles and do something about them, you will find that they have half the strength you think they have***

—Norman Vincent Peale

Read, listen and observe the lives of successful people and the obstacles they have overcome to convert failures into success.

28. ***Climbing steep hills requires slow pace at first***

—Shakespeare

Reward yourself for every small achievement or accomplishment.

29. ***So long as there is breath in me, that long I will persist. For new I know one of the greatest principles of success; if I persist long enough I will win***

—Og Mandingo

Accept the fact that work life in any organization will be full of ups and downs, pleasure and sorrow, appreciation and criticism.

30. ***There are only two words that will always lead you to success. Those words are Yes and No. Undoubtedly, you've mastered saying yes. So start practicing saying no. Your goals depend on it***

—Jack Cornfield

Take your own decisions and materialize on them.

31. ***The morality of compromise sounds contradictory. Compromise is usually a sign of weakness, or an admission of defeat. Strong men don't compromise, it is said and principles should never be compromised***

—Andrew Carnegie

Have firm principles, philosophies and moral values.

32. ***Listening is an attitude of the heart, a genuine desire to be with another which both attracts and heals***

—J. Isham

Listen to other employees' ideas, suggestions before giving your view.

33. ***There is more hunger for love and appreciation in this world than for bread***

—Mother Teresa

Respect and appreciate your subordinates, colleagues, bosses, team members and even your competitors and opponents.

34. ***What this power is I cannot say; all I know is that it exists and it becomes available only when a man is in that state of mind in which he knows exactly what he wants and is fully determined not to quit until he finds it***

—Alexander Graham Bell

Get involved in the task physically, mentally and emotionally.

35. ***Believe in yourself, in all you can do and for you, the deals will start to work in your favour. You need to be open to such deals, and they will come. I assure you***

—Ivana Trump

Fight till death for what you believe is right and fair.

36. ***Share your knowledge. It is a way to achieve immorality***

—Dalai Lama

Share your knowledge, skills and expertise.

37. ***Do more than what is required. What is the distance between someone who achieves the goals consistently and those who spend their lives and career merely following?***

—The extra mile - Gary Ryan Blair

Go the extra mile for your organization.

38. ***The problem with rat races is that even if you win, you are still a rat***

—Lily Tomlin

Never get involved in office politics.

39. ***What we see depends mainly on what we look for***

—John Lubbock

Know what is exactly expected from you in the organization and what you expect from the company.

40. ***Determination gives you the resolve to keep going in spite of the roadblocks that lay before you***

—Denis Waitley

Have contingency plan is B and C in case of emergency.

41. ***I believe that being successful means having a balance of success stories across many areas of your life. You can't truly be considered successful in your business life if your home life is shambled***

—Zig Ziglar

Have a balanced personal and professional life.

Finally, remember the fact that no external forces can motivate or demotivate us. Success and failure depend on us. Hence, to succeed, we need a strong will-power, fortitude, a positive attitude and perspective towards life.

Hence, self-motivation is enormously significant in every one's life. Despite the importance of self-motivation several myths still persist. It is important to identify these universal myths about employee motivation and find a suitable solutions for it.

Research has identified that there is an inverse relationship between reality and myth. A good leader identifies these old myths and tries to blast them as soon as possible.

40 Workplace Myths

40 myths that find place in the mind of every employee in an organization. Remember they are myths and have no realism attached.

1. Money is the greatest motivator.
2. Fear always works.
3. If they are not administered personally, most human resources will avoid work.
4. I can make everyone happy.
5. Delegation is dangerous.
6. I can never say "No".
7. Never trust your staff.
8. Training is expensive.
9. All employees hate work.
10. I can never accept my mistakes.
11. Most employees have an aversion for their bosses.
12. I can never accept my defeat.
13. I know everything about my job.
14. I can do everything and anything.
15. I can never understand my recruits.
16. Never get emotionally involved in your task.
17. Unrealistic targets double employees' efforts.
18. I can't recognize when I am stressed.
19. To create a good work atmosphere, I need to break my bank balance.
20. To endure in today's intensely competitive market, companies should keep remuneration to the minimum.
21. The manager is the reason for employees' lack of motivation.

22. Discussions ignite arguments which can be risky.
23. Telling people they've done a good job makes them over confident.
24. If only I work 14 hours a day, I will be promoted.
25. My competitors can never match my performance.
26. Core principles should be flexible and molded as per our requirement.
27. Making mistakes is the sign of inefficiency.
28. Creativity is not my cup of tea.
29. I cannot take my own decisions.
30. All tasks are equally important.
31. All employees are same.
32. I bank too much on luck.
33. No matter how satisfactorily a boss motivates, no worker will be happy with him.
34. Employees who work more are unhappy than the ones who work less.
35. Motivating work force is short-term, temporary and once a life-time effort.
36. Human resource is the most unpredictable element of business.
37. Never share what you know.
38. It is difficult to align employee's goal with the organizational goals.
39. Nearly every employee emphasizes on quantity than on quality.
40. Some employees don't need motivation.

51 Rules to Motivate Yourself at the Workplace

Research shows that if a person receives a reward such as, bonus, incentives or appreciation, praise immediately after the performance of the desired task, his productivity increases and vice-versa.

This desire or the spark that enables an individual to achieve the targeted goal or objective is described as motivation. All employees in an organization are not always internally or externally motivated. Thus, the manager needs to mingle both the factors effectively and efficiently and maintain a balance between both.

Some of the motivational theories developed by various experts are drive reduction theory, cognitive dissonance theory created by leon festinger, hierarchy of human needs theory by Abraham Maslow, two factor theory developed by Fredrick Herzberg, ERG theory suggested by Clayton Alderfer, self-determination theory created by Edward Deci and Richard Ryan, Broad theories by Heinz Schuler and George C and Thornton III and Andreas Frintrup and Rose Mueller Hanson, goal setting theory developed by Douglas Vermeeren.

Have we ever thought why some of us have low self-motivation at a workplace? The reasons can be many, but the good news is fortunately, self-motivation is a learnable skill and here are 51 golden rules and long-term motivational mantras.

"Genius is 1 per cent inspiration, and 99 percent perspiration"

—Thomas Edison

1. Hard work always pays

At workplace, we all undergo a certain amount of stress due to various reasons in the form of deadlines, competition, saturations, pressures, sorrows resulting in an unfavorable situation. However, we can not eliminate stress, however, we can learn to manage stress. Positive stress adds to anticipation and excitement. Nothing substantial is achieved without lot of hardship.

As Thomas Edison said, "Opportunity is missed by most people because it comes dressed in overalls and looks like work". Thus, most of us fail to recognize it. But neither there is any shortcut to success, nor is there any free lunch. Avoid being a mediocre and accept new challenging task by having a well-defined goal and a well-designed game plan. Miracles don't happen overnight; Rome was not built in a day. Your hard work for today determines your destiny for tomorrow as accomplishment of desired target gives immense satisfaction, pride and self-confidence.

> ***"It is one of the strange ironies of this strange life (that) those who work the hardest, who subject themselves to the strictest discipline, who give up certain pleasurable things in order to achieve a goal, are the happiest people."***
>
> *—Brutus Hamilton*

> ***"Success doesn't mean the absence of failures; it means the attainment of ultimate objectives. It means winning the war not every battle"***
>
> *—Edwin Bliss*

2. Be an optimist and develop a positive attitude

Our attitude determines how we look at our setback. It can be a stepping stone to success for a winner who never takes criticisms personally or it can be a stumbling block for a loser. Believe in yourself as it helps you to achieve the utmost of your ability and bring lots of success. 85 per cent of the time, according to a research Harvard University, when an individual gets a job or promotion is because of his positive attitude and the remaining 15 per cent is because of his intelligence and domain knowledge. This research demonstrates the importance of positive attitude in an individual's life.

As Helen Mac Inness rightly said, "Nothing is interesting, if you're not interested." Developing an optimistic and positive attitude requires a conscious efforts and determination. Try to change yourself before you change others because you cannot change everyone. Life is simple and wonderful. So enjoy it and be versatile to accept the reality. Face your difficulties to overcome it!

> ***"If you want to succeed, double your failure rate"***
>
> *—Tom Watson Sr., of IBM*

> ***"Every problem comes with an equal or greater opportunity"***
>
> *—Napoleon Hill, author of Think and Grow*

3. Analyze the opportunities

Make a SWOT (Strengths, Weaknesses, Opportunities and Threats) analysis of yourself to set your targets. Set goals that focuses on your strengths, minimizes your weaknesses, exploits the internal and external opportunities and controls the threats.

Daring ideas are like chessmen; moved forward, they may be beaten, but they may start winning a game. Based on your SWOT analysis, analyze each strategy independently, select the most appropriate one, implement the selected option, and then evaluate, monitor and take feedback of the executed strategy. For a smooth drive on a rough road, you must speed up at appropriate times. There are no shortcuts to success. Take the longer and right route to reach your target.

"Destiny is not a matter of chance, it is a matter of choice; it is not a thing to be waited for it is a thing to be achieved"

—William Jennings Bryan

"He slept beneath the moon, He basked beneath the sun, He lived a life of going to do, And died with nothing done"

—James Albery

4. Procrastination is the thief of time

Follow the principle of three most vital P's in life (Planning, Preparation and Practice) – utilize your time effectively, efficiently and productively by having a realistic goal with a time bound and a deadline, since delay of task adds to fear and anxiety. Experts have found that there can be various reasons of procrastination such as poor time management, anxiety, fear of failure/success/being alone, unrealistic expectation, etc. However, it can have internal effects like stress, guilt, lower productivity and creativity or external effects like punishment, fear of getting fired, demotion, etc.

"A good plan executed now is better than a perfect plan next week." – George S. Patton, Jr. To overcome the problem, recognize the reason for procrastination and develop suitable strategies to overcome it.

"Never leave till tomorrow, which you can do today"

—Benjamin Franklin

"Start by doing what is necessary, then what is possible, and suddenly you are doing the impossible"

—St. Francis of Assisi

5. Set your priorities

When something in life is critical and important, even though it may not always be fun, learn to accept it and like it. It always takes courage and strength to follow our ideas and views, but one must never be an emotional fool. Walt Disney feels, "Somehow I can't believe that there are any heights that can't be scaled by a man who knows the secrets of making dreams come true. This is a special secret; it seems to me that it can be summarized in four C's. They are Curiosity, Confidence, Courage and Consistency and the greatest of all is Confidence. When you believe in a thing, believe in it all the way, implicitly and unquestionably." Bring changes in yourself to change the outside world.

> ***"Many managers follow the notion of busy fools and confuse hard work with long hours. They think because they work 15-hours a day and forget their children's names, they must be bloody good managers. The best sales manager I have worked with never once worked beyond 5.30 pm"***
>
> *—Caspian Woods*

> ***"Most people give up just when they're about to achieve success. They quit on the one-yard line. They give up at the last minute of the game, one foot from a winning touchdown"***
>
> *—H. Ross Perot*

6. Don't quit

Problems/tragedies/obstacles in life can be disheartening and may result in frustration and then giving up. This may feel to be the simplest way. But winners never quit. They constantly analyze their strengths and weaknesses, develop various strategies to overcome the weaknesses and bounce back. Difficulties and problems make them stronger and a better fighter.

> ***"A man is a hero not because he is brave than anyone else, but because he is brave for 10 minutes longer"***
>
> *—Ralph Waldo Emerson*

> ***"Health, happiness and success depend upon the fighting spirit of each person. The big thing is not what happens to us in life — but what we do about what happens to us"***
>
> *—George Allen*

7. Have contigency plan B and C

Contingency plan also known as "back-up plans", "worst case scenario plans", "plan B and C", includes specific strategies, game plan, actions or tactics and are designed for the situations when the main plan goes wrong or fails due to any external reasons like change in the political, economic, social and technological reasons or internal factors such as change in management philosophy, mission, vision, human/physical/financial resource, etc.

Be prepared for such changes and have a well-defined strategy to overcome it. Tim Driskell once said that the day you decide to go out of these wild places and put yourself in these conditions, be responsible for yourself and those in your party. There are many requirements – good judgment, common sense, experience and leadership are just a few unexpected things can and do happen. Be prepared. Expect the unexpected. Always carry a bivvy sack on every climb. Be prepared to spend the night up here! Plan for the worst, but hope for the best!

"Don't confuse motion and progress. A rocking horse keeps moving but does not make any progress."

— Alfred A. Montapert

"If you work for a man, for heaven sake work for him"

—Kim Hubbard

8. Show commitment and devotion

Be proud of what you do for your living and the organization where you work. Never lose your self-respect, because he, who cannot respect his work, cannot expect others to respect him. All great tasks start with a small beginning. Commit yourself to achieve your organizational goals and devote the necessary time and efforts to achieve them. As a famous saying goes, an ounce of loyalty is worth more than a pound of cleverness.

If you're not committed it shows in your work, the way you manage customers, superiors and subordinates, which creates an unproductive, inefficient and pessimist environment. Encourage an environment where everyone encourages everyone else to be committed and devoted. Be a symbol of honesty and integrity.

"A duty which becomes a desire will ultimately become a delight"

—George Gritten

"The quality of a person's life is in direct proportion to their commitment to excellence, regardless of their chosen field of endeavour"

—Vince Lombardi

9. Dedication and discipline are vital components

"If discipline is practiced in every home, juvenile delinquency would be reduced by 95 per cent"

—J. Edgar Hoover

The same principles apply at our workplace as well. Winning is not an accident, it is the outcome of sincere dedication, discipline and whole-hearted effort and are the life-lines to achieve your goals. It takes lot of dedication, determination, devotion and discipline to work with integrity, honesty, and not to fall into pitfalls.

John Kennedy rightly said that it is a mark of character how well a person behaves when things are not going well. When things are going well for us, it is easy to be logical, kind and gracious. But when things aren't going well and we're under a lot a pressure, some people can't think clearly and snap at others around them, while others remain clear-headed and continue to treat others with respect. Adversity reveals a person's character.

"I like to work half a day. I don't care if it is the first 12 hours or the second 12 hours"

—Kammonns Wilson, CEO Holiday Inn

"Confidence gives you courage and extends your reach. It lets you take greater risk and achieve far more than you ever thought possible"

—Jack Welch

10. Role of self-confidence in achieving success

Our behaviour, attitude, body language, posture, presentation and communication skills show our self-confidence. Thus, it is extremely important in almost all aspects of our work, as there is direct relationship between self-confidence and success.

"Success is 99 per cent failure" – Soichiro Honda. People who lack self-confidence find it difficult to become successful but it can be learned, developed and build with consistent efforts. It is the key to sailing through any hardship. Say "I'm the Best" twice a day. How would you know how deep the ocean is or how high the mountain is until you start climbing... so don't fear in life.

"The only limit to our realization of tomorrow will be our doubts of today"

– Franklin D. Roosevelt

"Super achievers don't waste time in unproductive thoughts, esoteric thoughts, or catastrophic thoughts. They think constructively and they know that their level of thinking determines their success"

—Dr. Seymour Epstein

11. Set high standards

Compare and compete with your past performance to raise your standards higher each time you decide a goal to set an example for yourself and to make the task challenging but achievable.

Daniel H. Burnham said, "Make no little plans, they have no magic to stir men's blood... make big plans, aim high in hope and work." Increase in the standards/targets must be gradual and realistic, because if the targets are unrealistic, it adds to frustration and disappointment. Keep screening, scrutinizing and evaluating your goals to measure your outcome and capabilities.

"Brilliance is a standard, not a skill"

—Michael Heppell

"Dreams are a dime a dozen..., it's their execution that counts"

—Theodore Roosevelt

12. Be practical and realistic

To build high motivation within yourself, determine your greatest motivator — Is it money, incentives, bonus, commission, fame, recognition which are external and monetary benefits or non-financial motivators such as pride, sense of achievement, responsibility, belief, challenging and interesting job, respect which are internal.

The most powerful motivation, however comes from within. Making yourself aware of the negative consequences of not achieving the goals can have a big impact. Leo Rosten once said, "We see things as we are, not as they are." The grass always looks greener on the other side. Variety is the spice of life. Take power breaks if you are feeling burn-out as it's not the length but the depth in our work that counts.

"Success is the progressive realization of a worthy goal"

—Earl Nightingale

"Dealing with people is a lot like digging for gold. When you go digging for an ounce of gold you have to move tons of dirt. But when you go digging you don't go looking for the dirt, you go looking for the gold"

—Andrew Carnegie

(one of the largest steel manufacturers in United States)

13. Learn the art of man management

Delegate the task to the right person and then instruct them what should be done and what is expected from them. "Where the vision is one year, cultivate flowers. Where the vision is ten years, cultivate trees. Where the vision is eternity, cultivate people" — Oriental saying. Once the employees achieve their target — reward them and if they don't, let them learn from their mistakes to ensure that they don't repeat the same mistake again.

Control your anger as it can spill water on all your hard work. Jealousy leads to lapses in strong relationships. So stop thinking about others and things that doesn't matter. Common sense is not so common; learn to change yourself and not others.

"If people are coming to work excited... if they are making mistakes freely... if they are having fun... if they are concentrating on doing things, rather than preparing reports and going to meetings — then somewhere, you have leaders"

— Robert Townsend

"While one person hesitates because he feels inferior, the other is busy making mistakes and becoming superior"

—Henry C. Link

14. Never stop learning

As rightly said change is the only thing in the world which is constant. Always be flexible in life, look at the brighter side of change and be ready to move on. According to Professor Muhammad Yunus, "I simply wish to encourage you that, irrespective of what you have learnt in the school, always be ready to unlearn and relearn. Don't give up dreaming. If we all dream about a better world, I can guarantee you we'll get there." Regularly update yourself about the recent developments in your industry, organization, department and your team. Constantly identify the skills you need to acquire at workplace and then find out how you can acquire these skills.

"A manager's job is to create stability, and deal with reality. A leader's job is to stir emotion and set audacious, grandiose goals that shake the status quo. Too much management and you stagnate. Too much leadership and you get nowhere. Embrace the challenge of striking the balance. Do it well; and the result will surpass your wildest dreams"

—The Management and Leadership Network.

"The more I want to get some-thing done, the less I call it work"

—Richard Bach

15. Enjoy your work

Never play the blame game. It is better to deserve an honor and not have it than to have it and not deserve it.

Work is not always a pleasure or fun; but sometimes full of pain, compromises, sacrifices, disappointments, failures and commitments. An ideal combination of success comprises of five vital factors.

They are being charismatic, calm, cool, confident and composed. Happiness and sorrow go hand in hand and a winner faces it very strongly with their "go and get" attitude. Think out of the box; sometimes be a leader, an inventor, not just a follower, to conquer the world and to make your ordinary, routine work special and different.

"Success is not the key to happiness. Happiness is the key to success. If you love what you are doing, you will be successful"

—Albert Schweitzer

"Dignity is not in possessing but deserving"

—Mark Twain

"When I'd get tired and want to stop, I'd wonder what my next opponent was doing. When I could see them still working, I'd start pushing myself. When I could see him in my shower, I'd push myself harder"

—Dan Yable, Olympic Gold medalist in Wrestling

16. Learn from your competitors

Never underestimate your competitors. Spend some time in a day analyzing and evaluating their strengths, weaknesses, experiences, expertise, vision, target market, product/pricing/distribution/promotional and branding strategies.

"The illiterate of the 21st century will not be those who cannot read and write, but those who cannot learn, unlearn and relearn"

—Alvin Toffler

Thus, keep on examining their output and compare them with your result. Measure the deviations. If your output is less, find suitable measures to overcome the differences.

"Jealousy is... a tiger that tears not only its prey but also its own ragging heart"

—Michael Beer

"Any fact facing us is not as important as our attitude towards it, for that determines our success or failures"

—Norman Vincent Peale

17. Look for opportunity and not security

Opportunity is inversely proportional to security; the bigger the opportunity the lesser the security and more security means lesser opportunity.

"Don't wait for extraordinary opportunities. Seize common occasions and make them great. Weak men wait for opportunities; strong men make them."

—Orison Swett Marden

However, looking for opportunity involves taking calculated risk based on knowledge, past experience and expertise. Give yourself an opportunity to advance each time and reward yourself for your hard work.

"Luck I don't know anything about luck. I've never banked on it, and I am afraid of people who do. Luck to me is something else; hard work — and realizing what is opportunity and what is not"

—Lucille ball

"I don't know the key to success, but the key to failure is trying to please everybody"

—Bill Cosby

18. Never commit more than you can deliver

Don't aim at being liked, appreciated and accepted by everyone. As Michael de Montaige rightly remarked that there are some defeats more triumphant than victories.

Aim at a balanced mental, social, physical, financial, personal and spiritual life. It is always advisable to be good in all the six aspects, rather than being the best in any one of these. Promise and commit only when you can deliver.

> ***"Do you ever compromise on service? Do you cut corners, only partially fulfill, or even forget commitments? Exceptional service means keeping every commitment you make to customers. Period"***
>
> *—Mark Sanborn*

> ***"Associate yourself with people of good quality if you esteem your reputation, for it is better to be alone than to be in bad company"***
>
> *—George Washington*

19. Associate yourself with winners to become one

People with negative attitude know that hard work never kills anyone but feel, "why take a chance." Do you want to be one of them? Definitely NOT! Successful people, irrespective of their chosen field, have many qualities (personal as well as professional) in common, because for them, life is a journey and not a destination.

They follow Benedict Spinoza's principle in life, "... to become what we are capable of becoming is the only end of life." Thus, it is always recommended to stay away from people who spread negativity in the organization. So ally yourself with winners.

> ***"Average person puts only 25 per cent of his energy and ability into his work. The world takes off its hat to those who put in more than 50 per cent of their capacity, and stands on its head for those few and far between soul who devote 100 per cent"***
>
> *—Andrew Carnegie*

> ***"I hope I shall always possess firmness and virtue enough to maintain what I consider the most valuable of all titles, the character of an honest man"***
>
> *—George Washington*

20. Never compromise on your key values/principles

Insist on ethical and value oriented task rather than focusing only on theoretical information that we learn in school/colleges, which are more based on facts and figures. Trustworthiness, character, honesty, integrity, and fairness are the hallmark of greatness and determine the quality of a person. Be firm and fair on your core values and principles.

Calvin Coolidge once said that no person was ever honoured for what he received. Honor has been the reward for what he gave.

"Try not to become a success but rather try to become a man of value"

—Albert Einstein

"The critic is one who knows the price of everything and the value of nothing"

—Oscar Wilde

21. Never get disheartened by criticism

Don't let criticism dishearten you or demoralize you and distract you from your goals because everyone has the right to be wrong.

"I learned a long time ago never wrestle with a pig, you get dirty and besides, the pig likes it."

—Cyrus Ching

Learn to distinguish between an honest and dishonest critic; always listen and learn from an honest one and ask them for opinions and suggestions to enhance your productivity. So, the morale is to keep making mistakes, accept it, learn from it and don't repeat it. And during this process, you will find many critics. Understand their perception, but never get depressed. Success is to face failure and master them, but not absence of failure.

"A hammer shatters a glass but forges steel"

—A Russian Saying

"If you really want to succeed, form the habit of doing things that failures don't like to do"

—Anonymous

22. Get involved in the task mentally, physically and emotionally

Always do few things properly. People always remember our good work and not fast work. Be a good leader, rather than a good manager. That would make your team involved in the task and take pride and pleasure in the work. Be prepared for ups and downs, pleasure and sorrow each day and make your routine things exciting.

As Vaclav Havel believed that one should work for something because it is good, not just because it stands a chance to succeed. Be proud of what you do for your living. Never lose your self-respect, because he, who cannot respect his work, cannot expect others to respect him. But always take small breaks during long spell of work and engage your mind off stress by developing some hobbies, calling some old friends, surfing internet, listening to music, humorous tape or radio station you really enjoy.

> ***"Wealth without work, pleasure without conscience, knowledge without character, commerce without morality, science without humanity, religion without sacrifice, and politics without principles"***
>
> *—Mahatma Gandhi*

> ***"Responsibilities gravitate to the person who can shoulder them"***
>
> *—Elbert Hubbard*

23. Accept responsibity

As rightly said, success has many fathers, failure is an orphan. Hence, it is essential to accept accountability and responsibility when things don't go our way. One must be ready to take responsibility of failures as well and be prepared to say, "I take the responsibility... it was my fault" without making any excuses. It makes the person mature, acceptable, credible and empowered.

As Michael Korda, rightly, believed "Success on any major scale requires you to accept responsibility .... In the final analysis, the one quality that all successful people have is the ability to take on responsibility." Stop blaming your team members, seniors, management for your failures. One needs to accept complete responsibility for everything we are. Keep telling yourself at your workplace that, "I am responsible for this situation...; for my performance/growth", etc.

> ***"The price of greatness is responsibility"***
>
> *—Winston Churchill*

> ***"Tell me and I'll remember for an hour; show me and I'll remember for a day; but let me do it and I'll remember forever"***
>
> *—An old Chinese saying*

24. Have clearly defined responsibilities and duties

While performing duties, ensure that you have suitable authority and power to perform the task, since authorities and responsibilities are interdependent and interrelated.

Know what is expected from you, why it needs to be done, when it should be done with the deadline, where it has to be done, how it should be done, and who will help you to achieve your desired and specific results.

Never interfere with what you can't do. Accept changes and revolutions to face every challenge.

> ***"Do not confuse motion and progress. A rocking horse keeps moving but does not make any progress"***
>
> *—Alfred A. Motapert.*

> ***"Small people talk about other people, mediocre people talk about things, great people talk about ideas"***
>
> *—Anonymous*

25. Avoid criticizing others

People with negative attitude often blame the world for their failure. But honestly, we are responsible for our own success or failure. Life is a struggle and blaming others just adds fuel to fire. As rightly said, success is not to be measured so much by the position that one has reached in life as by the obstacles overcome, while trying to succeed.

Hence, never waste your time and efforts in unproductive and non-rewarding efforts such as criticizing your company, employers or employees publicly; try not to hurt anyone. Think before speaking and never speak without thinking. Never be a fault finder. Look for good things around. To succeed, try to achieve results with our own efforts.

> ***"The men who try to do something and fail are infinitely better than those who try to do nothing and succeed"***
>
> *—Lloyd Jones*

> ***"Share what you know and, more importantly, what you image with others. Lead them to discover their own truths. The way you live with your life is as powerful a teaching for others as what you say to them"***
>
> *—Tom Cowan*

26. Practice what you preach

"Practice" is to do things yourself first, whereas "Preach" means to suggest or advise someone else. Thus, you should do the activities yourself before you suggest people to do it. Share your knowledge, talent and skill.

> ***"Freedom is not procured by a full enjoyment of what is desired but by controlling the desire"***
>
> *—Epictetus*

Compliancy and tolerance does not always come naturally, they have to be developed, encouraged, nurtured and retained; thus make them an eternal element of life.

You can't expect integrity from others, if you are dishonest;

You can't expect punctuality from others, if you are never on time;

You can't expect courtesy from others, if your own behavior is rude;

You can't expect selflessness from others, if you are self-centered;

You can't expect humility from others, if you are arrogant;

You can't expect discipline from others, if you have no discipline;

You can't expect motivation from others, if you are demotivated;

Thus, our actions should be consistent with our words.

"An ounce of action is worth a ton of theory"

—Friedrich Engel's

"It is a given that all students will not be attracted to all teachers. It is also a given that respect, rather than being liked, is the hallmark of great teachers. But chances of achieving both are far greater through encouragement and empowerment than by saying, "call me by my first name"

—Dr. Marvin Marshall

27. Be firm, clear, fair, honest, loyal and straight forward

Have a clear, certain, determined, firm and fair direction, thought and approach in giving and getting instructions. To be loyal means to be reliable, consistent, and predictable in an unpredictable situation.

"Only the person having firm conviction and iron volition can attain strength and energy. At no stage of Karma does he ever hesitate."

—Rig Veda

Straightforwardness is about being obvious and explaining one's idea and opinion in a clear tone with kindness and calmness in simple, sweet and short sentences. Speak what you think is right.

"Make yourself an honest man and then you may be sure here is one rascal less in the world"

—Thomas Carlyle

"I consider my ability to arouse enthusiasm among the men the greatest asset I possess, and the way to develop the best that is in a man is by appreciation and encouragement"

—Charles Schwab

28. Be enthusiatic

Be your best friend. Start working early, get adequate sleep and rest to maintain your energy level. Occasionally, pamper yourself with a treat, week-ends off, trying out new combinations of food and clothes, as it helps to refresh our mind and body. Keep a check on your weight.

Excess weight increases the stress on our body, making it more prone to certain chronic diseases like obesity, fat, high blood pressure and cardiac disorder.

"Nothing great is ever achieved without enthusiasm"

—Ralph Waldo Emerson

"History has demonstrated that the most notable winners usually encountered heart-breaking obstacles before they triumphed. They won because they refused to become discouraged by their defeats"

—B. C. Forbes

29. Think Win-Win

Win/Win, Win/Lose, Lose/Win, Lose/Lose, Win, and Win/Win or No Deal are the six philosophies of negotiation or human interaction.

However, the most feasible and acceptable alternative is "win-win", since we aim at mutual benefits for both the parties involved in negotiation. It involves reasonable compromises, co-operation and sacrifices from both the parties.

It is a balancing act. As an age-old adage says, when we share sorrow, it divides; but when we share happiness, it multiples and help others. Thus, we automatically win. It also demonstrates the positive attitude of an individual to help others in spite of all the odds. "A kite rises highest against the wind, not with it" — Sir Winston Churchill

"Whatever the mind of man can conceive and believe, the mind can achieve"

—Napoleon Hill

"He who would learn to fly one day must first learn to stand and walk and run"

—Friedrich Nietzsche

30. Be a part of the team and not apart from the team

Always use statements like "We did it", "We deserved it" rather than "I did it" or "I deserved it." Try and celebrate your team's success together.

Never try to do a role of your other team members. Understand your strengths/weaknesses and your role in achieving the results. Always do what you are best at and avoid the rest. Listening is also a participative act. Listen to ideas, views, opinions, suggestions, creativity of others to develop team spirit and loyalty. Edmund Burke once said that for evil to flourish good people have to do nothing and evil shall flourish. Always support what you feel is right and needs encouragement. Resolve your differences immediately to avoid bitter relationships. Work harmoniously with others, but be laser-sharp.

"Egotism is the anesthetic that deadens the pain of stupidity"

—Knute Rockne

"A smooth sea never made a skillful mariner"

—An old English proverb

31. Find opportunities to face new and difficult situations

Keep ten minutes aside a day to formulate a forward looking plan and to answer few questions each day like, "how to generate more revenue", "how to reduce cost", "how to motivate my team", "how to upgrade my product", "how to enhance my company's image in the eyes of external people." Bernie Milano feels that the greatest advancements of this century, the light bulb, the airplane, and the computer, were created by innovators – people who imagined things that did not exist and asked why.

Being an outstanding employee requires a touch of this inventor's spirit, a determination to persistently strive to create value. The road to success is never smooth; so be tolerant since no hurdle/ no mountain is too high – a strong and silent attitude can eventually cause a volcano to erupt.

"You may be disappointed if you fail, but you will be doomed if you don't try"

—Beverley Sills

32. Did you know?

- **Abraham Lincoln** failed in business at the age of 21 and again at 24; was defeated in a legislative race at the age of 22; his girlfriend died when he was 26; lost a congressional race at age of 34; lost a senatorial race at the age of 45 and 49; failed in an effort to become the Vice-President at the age of 47; and was elected President of the United States at the age of 52.

- **Thomas Edison** failed approximately 10,000 times before he invented light bulbs.
- **Dhirubhai Ambani** started his career with A. Besse and Company at the age of 16, for a salary of Rs. 300/-. He returned to India in 1962 and with a capital investment of Rs. 1500/-, he started Reliance Commercial Corporation with the primary business to import polyester and export spices. When he died, Reliance had an annual gross turnover of around Rs. 75,000 crores.
- **Azim Premji** joined Wipro at the age of 21, immediately after his father's sudden demise with a vision to build an organization on the foundation of values. And the rest is history. He never looked back after that. Forbes rated him as the richest Indian from 1999 to 2005. As of October 6, 2007 his wealth is worth $13.6 billion.
- **Lakshmi Narayan Mittal**, one of the richest living in UK and Asia since 2005 and the fourth richest person on the earth with a total net worth of US $ 45 billion; the Chairman and CEO of ArcelorMittal, was born on June 15, 1950 in a small village called Sadulpur, in the Churu district of Rajasthan, India. He is presently living in Kensington, London, United Kingdom that he bought for $128 million, which was the most expensive home in the world at that time for over 14 years. Isn't it inspiring?

Read this inspiring stories/anecdotes/quotes: Keep some time aside in a day to read inspirational and motivating anecdotes of successful people such as Dhirubhai Ambani, Ratan Tata, Narayan Murty, Azim Premji, Lakshmi Mittal, who despite of several failures and serious limitations and weaknesses, have achieved success because of their burning desire to win.

The motivational thoughts of Bessie Stanley on success at the workplace:

To laugh often and much;

To win the respect of intelligent people and the affection of junior;

To earn the appreciation of honest critics and endure the betrayal of false friends;

To appreciate beauty, to find the best in others;

To leave the world a bit better, whether by a

healthy child, a garden patch or a redeemed social condition;

To know even one life has breathed easier

Because you have lived.

This is to have succeeded.

"A clear vision, backed by definite plans, gives you a tremendous feeling of confidence and personal power"

—Brain Tracy

33. Visualize what you want to achieve

Keep your focus on what you want to achieve and what you don't want to. Success is an ideal combination of hard work, talent, determination, dedication, devotion, discipline, will power, character, honestly, vision, and loyalty.

In addition to the above qualities, Napoleon Hill has mentioned three additional unbeaten combinations for success, i.e., patience, persistence and perspiration. Keep moving. Don't be irreplaceable. If you can't be replaced, you can't be promoted. Believing our heart takes courage and conviction, so don't hesitate to speak your mind but speak sensibly, firmly and sparingly.

"Great minds have purposes, others have wishes"

—Washington Irving

"One of the deepest desires of human being is the desire to be appreciated. The feeling of being unwanted is hurtful"

—William James

34. Appreciate and encourage others

Life is like an echo; if you treat others with respect and dignity, you will get back what you give. Acknowledge and appreciate the efforts of others to boost their morale. A work done for other is a task worth remembering for everyone, because our little effort also counts. It is always better to do something than nothing.

Understand that the team is a group of people who have their individual likes, dislikes, preferences, qualities, beliefs, opinions, ideas, suggestions and individuality. Hence, you need to understand and accept the capabilities, strengths and weaknesses of each team member and allow them to share their views and bring their contributions. As Casey Stengel once said that getting good players is easy, getting them to play together is the difficult part.

"The biggest disease today is not leprosy or tuberculosis but rather the feeling of being unwanted"

—Mother Teresa

"The harder you work, the luckier you get"

—Henry Ford

35. Luck... don't bank too much on it

Never completely surrender yourself to luck and completely attribute your success and failure to your fate. Winners believe in hard work, commitment, and dedication; losers believe in luck, fate, and destiny. Luck is the meeting point between hard work and destiny.

As someone rightly said,
He worked by day,
And toiled by night.
He gave up play,
And some delight.
Dry books he read,
New things to learn.
And forges ahead,
Success to earn.
He plodded on with,
Faith and pluck;
And when he won,
Men called it luck.

"I am a great believer in luck, and I find he harder I work, the more I have of it"

—Thomas Jefferson

"Life is like a ten-speed bicycle. Most of us have gears we never use"

—Charles Schultz

36. Half-hearted efforts produces no outcome

Accomplishment of desired task with full consistency, enthusiasm, excitement, challenge, dedication and passion is the most powerful motivator. As Albert Einstein once said, "I think I used about 25 per cent of my intellectual capability during my life." Half-hearted attempt endanger productivity, creativity, competitiveness and can never lead to your desired target. However, one can identify the reasons for lower productivity by identifying why the task does not achieve a whole-hearted effort, what is causing low productivity, what can be done about it, how it can be eliminated in the future. Recognize when you are stressed. Burn-out reduces productivity and also saps your energy.

"The biggest mistake we could ever make in our lives is to think we worked for anybody but ourselves"

—Brain Tracy

"A group becomes a team when each member is sure enough of himself and his contribution to praise the skills of the others"

—Norman Glass Shidle

37. Be a part of the answer and not a part of the problem

See an answer for every problem and not a problem for every answer. A problem is an obstacle that makes it difficult for us to achieve our mission. Every problem needs a solution. Thus, an individual needs to decide whether he wants to add fuel to fire by being a part of the unfavorable situation/circumstances or try to find a reply/solution to the problem by being a part of the response/answer; i.e. whether he is a problem creator or problem solver. Impossible itself means, "I'm Possible."

Life is hard by the yard, But by the inch, It's a cinch.

—Gean Gorden

"Bring me solutions, not problems"

—Margaret Thatcher

"We cannot help ourselves without helping others
We cannot enrich our lives without enriching others
We cannot prosper without bringing prosperity to others"

—Janette Cole

38. Volunteer your time and efforts to help your subordinates

In any organization, all activities are inter-connected and inter-dependent on each other. Thus, volunteering our time and efforts in helping others can really make a big difference.

"In helping others, we shall help ourselves, for whatever good we give out, completes the circle and comes back to us."

—Flora Edwards

If you know more about a particular subject; share it with your subordinates, sharing and helping others boost our self-confidence, reduces stress, and increases our subject knowledge.

"When you are good to others, you are best to yourself"

—Benjamin Franklin

"If you think you can or if you think you can't, you are right"

—Henry Ford

39. Dominate your thoughts/ ideas/views, but never let them dominate you

Let your ideas consciously decide your goals based on your ability and intelligence. Encourage ideas, opinions, and feedback from others. Listen to their views, analyze them and then take your own decision rationally. As said by A. Harvey Block ideas that come out of most brainstorming sessions are usually superficial, trivial, and not very original. They are rarely useful.

The process, however, seems to make uncreative people feel that they are making innovative contributions and that others are listening to them. Do what you believe in to gain courage, strength and confidence. Life is very unpredictable, unimaginable, undeterred, and full of risk, fun and adventure but with proper planning, one can reach any limit and climb the mountain.

"What a man thinks of himself that is what determines or rather indicates, his fate"

—Henry David Thoreau

"It is amazing how much you can accomplish if you don't care who gets the credit"

—Harry Truman

40. Create a positive, congenial, enjoyable and favourable work environment to increase your performance and productivity

Encouraging a kind, loyal, cooperative and an honest work environment generates loyalty and team spirit. "The leaders who work effectively, it seems to me, never say "I". And that's not because they have themselves not to say "I". They don't think "I". They think "We", they think "Team".

Understanding their job is to make the team function. They accept responsibility and don't sidestep it, but, "we" gets the credit.... This is what creates trust, what enables you to get the task done." All days will not be alike; there will be moments of frustration, tiredness, boredom, idleness and irritation. Be ready to tackle them. Listen what others say if you want them to hear you.

> ***"A group becomes a team when each member is sure enough of himself and his contribution to praise the skills of the others"***
>
> *—Norman Glass Shidle*

> ***"I don't know what kind of people you're used to dealing with. Nobody tells me what to do in my place"***
>
> *—Karen Allen in Raiders of the Lost Ark*

41. Take your own decisions

Be decisive and bold. Taking your own, independent decision means coming to a logical conclusion after analyzing various alternatives and information available. There are various tools and techniques, such as Pareto analysis, Grid analysis, Cost/Benefit analysis, Decision Tree, etc., available with an individual. Have courage and confidence to take your own decisions even if you are wrong sometimes.

If you make mistakes, accept it, learn from it and don't repeat it. As rightly said, the man who makes no mistakes usually does not make anything.

> ***"Sometimes you just have to follow your intuition"***
>
> *—Bill Gates*

> ***"No one is less ready for tomorrow than the person who holds the most rigid beliefs about what tomorrow will contain"***
>
> *—Watts Wacker, Jim Taylor and Howard Means*

42. Always expect the unexpected

Prepare yourself for unpredictable incidents/accidents and be ready to handle them. Be innovative, proactive, and adaptive to accept new ideas and challenges and also to break the monotony.

Abraham Lincoln once said that the best thing about the future is that it only comes one day at a time. Depending on the situation, a successful manager takes his decision and adapts his management style accordingly. They adopt the old carrot and stick approach - reward the workers with monetary/non-monetary motivation to enhance their productivity and to celebrate your success.

> ***"Each one of us should know what our customers expect before they know it"***
>
> *—Dinesh K. Gupta and Ashok Jambhekar*

> ***"Happiness is an attitude. We either make ourselves miserable, or happy and strong. The amount of work is the same"***
>
> *—Francesca Reigler*

43. Keep smiling, be kind and gentle

Keep smiling, be enthusiastic, cheerful and considerate; it's contagious. Laughter lowers blood pressure and reduces hypertension.

> ***"Laugh and even the birds laugh with you, laughter is prayer. If you can laugh, you have learnt how to pray. Don't be serious. Only a person, who can laugh, not only at others but at himself also, can be religious."***
>
> *—Osho Rajneesh*

It helps to kill stress. For every ten minutes you are stressed, you lose 600 seconds of happiness. A healthy mind dwells in a happy and healthy body. Inculcate the habit of forgive and forget, and don't hold grudges. Smile, as it is priceless.

> ***"Rudeness is the weak man's imitation of strength"***
>
> *—Eric Hoffer*

> ***"Success seems to be connected with action. Successful people keep moving. They make mistakes, but they don't quit"***
>
> *—Conrad Hilton*

44. Learn from past mistakes

Bradley G. Richardson compares a career setback with a romance gone bad. He adds that if you don't learn from your mistakes, you're doomed to repeat them, most likely in your next job. Many professionals are so eager to flee from a bad job or fearful of being jobless, they jump from one mismatched job to the next, just like some people do in their personal relationships.

If you've been knocked down but haven't looked at what caused you stumble, you're setting yourself up to fall again. Thus, we learn that when we make any mistake, we must willingly accept it, and learn from it, so that we don't repeat it again. Never regret your past, don't worry about future. Simply think of the day that is today. Don't be stubborn. Don't try the same route where you once slipped.

"We are what we repeatedly do. Excellence is not an act but a habit"

—Aristotle

"On the journey to life's highway, keep your eyes upon the goal. Focus on the donut, not upon the hole"

—Anonymous

45. Leverage on your strengths and past successes

Never let your past failures/break downs/weaknesses worsen your self-confidence. Use your strengths to offset your weaknesses. Once you realize your weaknesses, don't waste your time and efforts. Begin to work on them and improve yourself.

"Aim at the sun and you may not reach it; but your arrow will fly far higher than if you had aimed at an object on a level with yourself"

— Joel Hawes

For example, if you realize that, in your organization, your computer knowledge is strong, but probably your weakness is communication skills, find out whether your weakness is affecting your productivity or output. If yes, start improving it. Focus on your core competencies, count on your strengths and understand:

What are you good at? Where, why, and when you need improvement? How can I improve? Whose help or advice should I ask for to improve myself? Experience is the best teacher. It helps you to find solutions of several unanswered questions.

"Obstacles are those frightful things you see when you take your eyes off your goal"

—Henry Ford

"Almost everyone is born with the capacity to be creative, but few realize it and such skills are often neglected or untapped. Lateral thinking is all about thinking "outside the box" breaking out of familiar thought patterns and coming up with new possibilities. It is one of the keys to improving creativity"

—Lloyd King

46. Be creative, innovative and constructive

Keep your eyes and ears open for any innovative ideas/suggestions. Keep on analyzing the opportunities to do the same thing in a dynamic, relaxed and better way. A common workplace axiom states that if you do what you have done, you will always get what you have got.

Develop an open and two way channel of upward and downward communication to encourage trust, respect, ideas, views, opinions, suggestions and constructive criticism. Mould yourself according to the environment and situation. Never fear making mistakes when trying to implement new ideas.

> ***"The best and the most beautiful things in the world cannot be seen or even touched. They must be felt with the heart"***
>
> *—Helen Keller*

> ***"I have never had a policy. I have simply tried to do what seemed best each day, as each day came"***
>
> *—Abraham Lincoln*

47. Maintain a "to-do-list" and a "planner" to utilize time effectively

Keep evaluating your long-term and short-term goals for a forward looking plan.

> ***"I find it fascinating that most people plan their vacations with better care than they plan their lives. Perhaps, that is because escape is easier than change"***
>
> *—John Rohn*

> ***"Patience creates confidence, decisiveness, and a rational outlook which eventually leads to success"***
>
> *—Brian Adams*

48. Patience and persisitance are the key motivators

Stress and challenges at workplace in any form requires a critical combination of patience and persistence. Prepare yourself for the success and failure, ups and downs, surprises and frustration, happiness and sorrow, changes and consistency at your workplace, since all days may not be alike. In times of failures, frustration, and sorrow, quitting or giving up seems to be the most feasible option.

However, in the long run, patience and persistence are the ideal survival mantra. As Calvin Coolidge feels, nothing will take the place of persistence. Talent will not: nothing is more common than unsuccessful people with talent. Genius will not: unrewarded genius is a proverb. Education will not: the world is full of educated derelicts. Persistence and determination alone are omnipotent.

"Everyone should be quick to listen, slow to speak and slow to become angry"

—James 1:19

"Your goals should be realistic and achievable. If you set yourself unrealistic goals, you are only setting yourself up for the possibility of failure and disappointment. Larger tasks should be broken down into smaller, more manageable ones. This will make the larger projects seem less daunting. It will also give you a sense of achievement on completion. When calculating how long you will need to complete a task, leave extra time in case the work takes longer than expected. This will relieve the time pressure"

—Barbara Nance

49. Keep in mind your personal and professional short-term and long-term goals for "big picture" thinking

At the end of each day, analyze the effectiveness of the task done, the decisions taken and the work assigned with deadlines. Evaluate areas of improvement for the next day and strategies to overcome those weaknesses and execution of that well-defined plan.

"Making mistakes simply means you are learning faster"

—Weston H. Agor

Based on the organizational goals, decide and prepare your objectives. Your objectives must be clear, simple, easy to understand, and well supported by facts, figures and reliable data. Preparations boost our self-confidence, helps us to identify mistakes, rectify them and learn from them.

"I have found that being honest is the best technique I can use. Right up front, tell people what you're trying to accomplish and what you're willing to sacrifice to accomplish it"

—Lee Iacocca

"It is better to have enough ideas for some of them to be wrong, than to be always right by having no ideas at all"

—Edward de Bono

50. Encourage constructive criticism

Be open in giving and receiving criticism, feedback and ideas, since it helps us to know what we are doing wrong and where we need improvement. Listen to others, but follow your heart.

As Earl Nightingale feels, "Don't let the fear of the time it will take to accomplish something stand in the way of your doing it. The time will pass anyway; we might just as well put that passing time to the best possible use." Take five minutes a day to encourage positive criticism. Discuss but don't argue, since a steady discussion can result in an intelligent solution. Be an active and good listener. Simultaneously, learn the art of differentiating between an honest and sincere appreciation and flattering.

> ***"Study as if you were to live forever; live as if you were to die tomorrow"***
>
> *—Mahatma Gandhi*

> ***"Everyone has a will to win but very few have the will to prepare to win"***
>
> *—Vince Lombardi*

51. Always use positive words like "I can", "I will", "I am able", and "it is possible"

Wikipedia defines motivation as the set of reasons that determines one to engage in a particular behaviour. Thus, to believe in oneself and be internally motivated, one needs to develop and maintain an attitude within oneself that creates a favourable, acceptable, optimist, confident and conscious mind, and leads to success and keeps them focused on the goal.

As someone has rightly said, tell yourself that "I like things to happen. And if they don't happen, I like to make them happen" and repeat it several times in a day to boost your morale and self-confidence.

> ***"No one can make you feel inferior without your permission"***
>
> *—Eleanor Roosevelt*

May You Have

May you have...
Enough happiness to keep you sweet,
Enough trials to keep you strong,
Enough sorrow to keep you human,
Enough hope to keep you happy;
Enough failure to keep you humble,
Enough success to keep you eager,
Enough friends to give you comfort,
Enough wealth to meet your needs;
Enough enthusiasm to look forward,
Enough faith to banish depression,
Enough determination to make each day better than yesterday.

—Unknown

11 Ways to Motivate Employees

You cannot bring prosperity by discouraging thrift.
You cannot strengthen the weak by weakening the strong.
You cannot enrich the poor by impoverishing the rich.
You cannot establish sound security on borrowed money.
You cannot help the wage earner by pulling down the wage payer.
You cannot build character and courage by taking away man's initiative and independence.
You cannot further the brotherhood of man by inciting class hatred.
You cannot keep out of trouble by spending more than you earn.
You cannot help men permanently by doing for them what they could and should do themselves"

—Abraham Lincoln

Managers have to perform different functions such as planning, organizing, directing, staffing, co-ordination, controlling etc., however, properly motivating the workforce is the most multifaceted, versatile and complex activity.

Each employee needs a separate motivational tool, thus a manager needs to understand what motivates an employee, as the skill to motivate employees to yield maximum output is the core function of management.

Motivation requires a tailored approach to each workers wants and requirements. This is because a motivational tool for one staff member may be a demotivating factor for another. Senior managers are responsible for motivating their work-force for their retention, development, progression and better performance, as sincerity, integrity, truthfulness, devotion, reliability, dependability, faithfulness, constantly survive in an environment of high positive motivation.

Hence, the manager needs to ally the organizational objectives with the goals of the employees. A manager needs to consider the employee's age, needs, life phase before deciding any motivational tool.

Here are some of the key factors that motivate workforce.

1. Attractive Salary/wages

"Money is human kind's greatest invention. Money doesn't discriminate. Money doesn't care whether a person is poor, whether a person comes from a good family, or what his skin colour is. Anybody can make money."

—Takafumi Horie

Each and everyone need money for survival and endurance. Thus, employees would like to earn reasonable salaries/wages because they view money as an elementary and essential encouragement for functioning. Attractive salary is always a key aspect in motivating the staff. In fact, a concrete salary package is generally the best motivational technique.

However, the compensation package must be at par or higher than the industry standards to attract and retain competitive candidates, and maintain an energetic and motivated work environment. This is because employees mostly compare their package within and outside the organization for similar positions, job descriptions, qualifications and work experience.

If the management wants to alter or modify their company's policies, procedures or change any course of action, strategy, guidelines, etc., they need to recognize the importance and significance of such alteration or revolutions and compensate the employees adequately and proportionally to match their efforts and involvement to the change. As Alexander Hamilton has rightly said, "In the main, it will be found that a power over a man's support (salary) is a power over his will".

2. Allowances

"Study until 25, investigate until 40, profession until 60, at which age I would have him retired on a double allowance."

—William Osler

While salary is one of the most appreciated methods to encourage employees, there are several other monetary tools as well. One of them is an attractive allowance plan. An allowance is explained by Wikipedia as an amount of money set aside for a designated purpose. Pension plan, sick leave, maternity/paternity leave, annual holiday, conveyance, lunch coupons, leave travel, house rent, educational, medical reimbursement, gratuity, travel, over-time, recreational benefits are some of the monetary allowances for employees.

However, such allowances may vary from company to company, department to department and employee to employee. Before designing an allowance plan, the management must decide whether they want to give monthly, bi-monthly, quarterly, half yearly or annual allowances to the staff. However, the employee must never doubt the importance of allowances, even if it is just a fraction of an overall remuneration package for workers. William Makepeace Thackeray, an Indian born English novelist and author of "*Vanity Fair*" once stated, "Though small was your allowance, you saved a little store: and those who save a little shall get a plenty more".

3. Bonus

> ***"A lot of companies make diversity a part of their performance goals against which an executive gets paid. Just as you have to make a certain sales number, you have to make a diversity number to get your bonus."***
>
> *—Vernon Jordan*

The word "bonus" is derived from a Latin word "bonum", which means good. It is something given in addition to the salary as an extra payment to the employees in appreciation for their good performance. Whenever a listed company earns profit, under the Bonus Payment Act, 1965 it has to declare bonus to the employees. Thus, a bonus is only declared by the management if the organization is profitable for a stipulated time period.

Bonus is not always about money. It is sometimes an admiration and an additional benefit to employees individual and team's efforts and hard-work. "My dream was to be known as a writer and to be able to produce at least one book that would be read by people."

4. Incentives

> ***"Everyone who's ever taken a shower has an idea. It's the person who gets out, dries off, and does something about it who makes a difference"***
>
> *—Nolan Bushnell*

Monetary payment in addition to the salary, to appreciate and acknowledge the efforts of the employees is termed as incentive. For example, performance award, attendance award, etc. It is also explained as a financial or non-financial reward given to the worker for his valuable contribution to organizational success.

Such reward encourages employees to perform better than other. Straight Piece Rate (where the workers is paid for the quantity he produces in a day), Straight Piece Rate with a guaranteed base wage (here the employee is remunerated for the quantity decided by the management even if the productivity is less than the desired target but if the output exceeds the determined target the management adopts the earlier method), Halsey Plan (here the manager adopts the following modus operandi: W= R.T + (P/100) (S-T) where W= Wage of human resource, R= wage rate, T= actual time taken to complete task, P= % of profit shared with employees and S = Standard time allowed) and Rowan Plan (where W- R.T {(S-T)/S}. R.T is the formula adopted) are different types of incentive programs available with the employer. "Performance related Incentive Program" is the best method as it creates a congenial work environment.

However, the plan needs to be specially made according to the productivity of each employee. Incentive motivation is a "carrot" – the employee will work because there is a reward in the front. Earl of Beaconsfield believes that the secret of success in life is for a man to be ready for his opportunity when it comes.

5. Fair Treatment to Employees

> ***"We are dedicated to promoting a culture of respect, which values diversity and fosters an appreciation for the rights and individual differences of others"***
>
> *—Prince Edward School's belief*

Employees expect firm, fair and decent treatment, co-operation, honesty, affection, and two-way effective communication from their employer. Recognition of effective work enhances the performance of the employee and cultivates loyalty and team spirit. It makes the employees physically, mentally and emotionally involved in the task.

The management must learn to give immediate appreciation to the deserving employee. Appreciation is free, 100 per cent effective, comparative simple (than financial rewards), less time and efforts consuming and long lasting. It's an ongoing process and should be done on continuous basis. It helps to build their self-confidence and inspires others to perform well. Acknowledgement can be in the form of small rewards (like a box of sweets/ chocolate, time-off, lunch coupons, gifts or even trophy or certificate.) The management must praise their employees and give sincere appreciation and just not flatter them. As Jonathan Swift rightly supposed, "It's an old maxim in the schools that flattery's the food of fools, yet now and then you men of wit will condescend to take a bit".

6. Career Development and Growth

> ***"The future depends on what we do in the present"***
>
> *—Mahatma Gandhi*

"The study of Career Development looks at:

- How individuals manage their careers within and between organizations.
- How organizations structure the career progress of their members, it can also be tied into succession planning within some organizations".

Every organization needs an effective career development plan for their employees to retain the best talent. For an employee, career development is the route to growth and better opportunities. The manager perceives it as retention and encouragement device. Promotion, induction, training, job enrichment, job enlargement, job rotation, succession planning are some of the career development programmes.

Management must encourage ideas, views, opinions, suggestions, feedback and creativity from employees because nurturing and fostering the professional career of the employee is the duty and responsibility of the top management. It comes from top down.

Induction, regular trainings, management development programmes, orientation, in-house seminars, etc., are necessary to upgrade and update the knowledge and skills of the employees. Management must regularly update their employees on the latest inventions/creations in the industry, new technology, terminology and methodology. An employer must allow its employees to make mistakes and learn from them but ensure that the mistake is not repeated.

Similarly employees must also remember John F. Kennedy's words that our privileges can be no greater than our obligations. The protection of our rights can endure no longer than the performance of our responsibilities.

7. Congenial Work Conditions

> ***"You need to be aware of what others are doing; applaud their efforts, acknowledge them in their pursuits. When we all help one another, everybody wins"***
>
> *—Jim Stovall*

In a positive and optimist environment, an average employee's productivity increases. Whereas, in a negative surrounding, a productive employees output decrease. An optimistic environment fosters positive attitude among workers, which results in a pleasing, energizing, inspiring, productive, congenial, loyal work culture.

Proper safety standards, ventilation, lightening, stationary, fire drills, first aid are few requirements to create a decent work environment. These factors won't increase productivity but their absence can decrease efficiency. In a nutshell, the work condition must be safe, secure, pleasant and comfortable.

Employees must periodically celebrate their department/team's success to make the employees feel that their hard work, effort, will-power has been rewarded. Jeanette Cole believes that we cannot help ourselves without helping others.

We cannot enrich our lives without enriching others. We cannot prosper without bringing prosperity to others.

8. Job Security

> ***"Strong managers who make tough decisions to cut jobs provide the only true job security in today's world. Weak managers are the problem. Weak managers destroy jobs."***
>
> *—Jack Welch*

If the employee is cynical, bored, disinterested or distrustful about his future or pessimistic of being promoted or a salary raise in the company, he might lose his self-motivation and his self-confidence and productivity decreases.

Hence, the employee must be well aware of the opportunities and growth potential ahead for them in the organization. This leads to satisfaction among employees and this satisfaction results in pleasure and delight in the task and it is the vital ingredient in a successful recipe.

Further, even if the company has made some employees jobless, forced an employment freeze or demoted, transferred or removed people, it can have a substantial effect on employees' motivation and result in doubts, qualms, worries and uncertainty among work-force. It is vital that the employees feel secure, protected, harmless, safe and sound for the company. But, maintaining a risk free secure environment is the responsibility of both the employee as well as the employer.

Anthony Robbins, an American advisor to leaders, quoted that most people never feel secure because they are always worried that they will lose their job, lose the money they already have, lose their spouse, lose their health, and so on. The only true security in life comes from knowing that every single day, you are improving yourself in some way, that you are increasing the caliber of who you are and that you are valuable to your company, your friends, and your family."

9. Employee Participation in Key Decision-making

"One of the deepest desires of human being is the desire to be appreciated. The feeling of being unwanted is hurtful"

—William James

Occasionally, the management should have one-on-one meeting with each employee to get their valuable feedback, contribution and inputs in vital resolutions and verdicts. This helps the management to set realistic achievable goals and understand the expectations and interest of the employees which makes them feel good and builds a long-term interpersonal relationship. Participation helps to create devotion, trustworthiness, reliability, commitment, enthusiasm and loyalty.

Employee participation has two major advantages:

First, the employees feel they are treated with respect, equality, justice and evenhandedness. Secondly, the organization gets diversified views and opinions and save them from being entangled in accusation of employees rights to fair treatment by the employer in the work-place. It is in fact a "win-win" situation for all.

Hence, an employee must have a right to speak what they think is right. However, it may look very calculative, if not done genuinely and honestly. If a decision goes wrong, the management should not play the blame game and use their employees as an excuse. As Edward de Bono said on one occasion, "It is better to have enough ideas for some of them to be wrong, than to be always right by having no ideas at all".

10. Delegation of Authority and Power

"Share what you know and, more importantly, what you imagine with others. Lead them to discover their own truths. The way you live is as powerful a teaching for others as what you say to them"

—Tom Cowan

Management must clearly define the duties and responsibilities of each employee and provide the necessary authority and power to perform those duties. Simultaneously, they must ensure that the employee gets the best assets to execute the task in a quicker, better, and faster way. Delegation with clearly defined duties and authorities avoid confusion. But, it requires a clear understanding of the employee's strengths, weaknesses, likes and dislikes.

Delegating responsibility and authority to perform certain activity allows manager to concentrate on important task rather than routine activity. This saves a substantial amount of time and efforts for managers. It also boosts the morale of the employee since they feel trusted and appreciated. Manager needs to recognize the basic purpose, foundation, and utility of delegating authority and power.

Inappropriately allotted responsibilities without proper authority can lead to misunderstanding, disorder, puzzlement and uncertainty. Hence, the management must first identify the workers who can handle extra responsibility based on their competency, strength and weakness. For this, it is necessary to assign the right task to the right person. Elbert Hubbard stated that Responsibilities gravitate to the person who can shoulder them.

11. Fear

> ***"The answer, maybe, is going out and doing rather than waiting. If you wait, life will probably pass you by. But if you go out and do the things you want to, take the risks you fear, you may just find that everything slots into place."***
>
> *—Rob E. Geraghty*

Fear of punishment, demotion, criticism or removal can sometimes be a powerful instrument to bring the employees back down to earth and cultivate positive attitude as the human resource has the fright of losing, probably their current designation, incentives or even their job.

It can also be fear of failure, letdown, disappointment, embracement, humiliation, awkwardness or discomfiture. Fear motivation is instant, immediate, and direct and gets the task completed rapidly and speedily. Perhaps, it is the most supportive motivational tool in short run because not all nervousness, concern, fretfulness and angst are bad. But, the manager must use this tool carefully as at time Fear motivation can route to negativity among employees which can further demolish their self-confidence and spirit. Hence, the management must have an art/skill of maximizing output with minimum fear motivation. The negativity of fear concurs to Yoda's sentiment: "Fear is the path to the dark side. Fear leads to anger. Anger leads to hate. Hate leads to suffering".

The Most Beautiful Flower

The park bench was deserted as I sat down to read
beneath the long, straggly branches of an old willow tree.
Disillusioned by life with good reason to frown,
for the world was intent on dragging me down.
And if that weren't enough to ruin my day,
A young boy out of breath approached me,
All tired from play. He stood right before me with his head tilted down
And said with great excitement, "Look what I found!"
In his hand was a flower, and what a pitiful sight,
With its petals all worn — not enough rain, or too little light.
Wanting him to take his dead flower and go off to play,
I faked a small smile and then shifted away.
But instead of retreating he sat next to my side
And placed the flower to his nose and declared with overacted surprise,
"It sure smells pretty and it's beautiful, too.
That's why I picked it; here, it's for you."
The weed before me was dying or dead.
Not vibrant of colours: orange, yellow or red.
But I knew I must take it, or he might never leave.
So I reached for the flower, and replied, "Just what I need."
But instead of him placing the flower in my hand,
He held it mid-air without reason or plan.
It was then that I noticed for the very first time
That weed-toting boy could not see: he was blind.
I heard my voice quiver; tears shone in the sun
As I thanked him for picking the very best one.
"You're welcome," he smiled, and then ran off to play.
Unaware of the impact he'd had on my day.
I sat there and wondered how he managed to see
A self-pitying woman beneath an old willow tree.
How did he know of my self-indulged plight?
Perhaps from his heart, he'd been blessed with true sight.
Through the eyes of a blind child, at last I could see.
The problem was not with the world; the problem was me.
And for all of those times I myself had been blind,
I vowed to see the beauty in life,
And appreciate every second that's mine.
And then I held that wilted flower up to my nose
And breathed in the fragrance of a beautiful rose
And smiled as I watched that young boy,
Another weed in his hand,
About to change the life of an unsuspecting old man.

—Unknown

20 Quick Non-monetary Ways to Motivate

In today's modern business world, "money" is always a chief motivating aspect and a good salary package is vital to attract and retain workforce. However, many times, it is not an effective tool. A constant superlative solution in form of bonus, incentives, and allowances gets elapsed quickly.

The management is hardly ever able to monetarily compensate recruits as much as they expect. But, by providing non-monetary motivations, they can successfully encourage their staff and helps them to effectively manage their time. Motivating the workforce without monetary incentives is tough and challenging, but it can be successfully achieved with proper time management and other motivational techniques.

These 20 tools can be adopted by employers to boost their employee's confidence and spirit.

This chapter clearly reveals that there are many non-monetary motivational tools, besides monetary rewards to create employees reliability, trust-worthiness, dependability and allegiance.

1. Appreciation of Good Work

> ***"We are all motivated by a keen desire for praise, and the better a man is, the more he is inspired by glory"***
>
> *—Cicero*

When your employee achieves a desired target, it is vital to acknowledge his efforts. So, appreciate employees at that very moment when they accomplish the desired objective, since positive remarks from seniors are very encouraging. Stress on their positive aspects rather than their negative points.

Try to constantly highlight their achievements and accomplishments and not their faults, errors and blunders. In a month, the management can provide a "wooden trophy/plate" to the most productive, creative, innovative and inventive employee to reward his achievement or even generously congratulate the worker by giving him a round of applause and show appreciation. With limited or no appreciation for work, employees become irritated, upset, discouraged and annoyed.

Hence, a thank-you note or letter of appreciation, recognition or achievement mentioned on a company's circular, news-sheet, bulletin or notice-board can be a good motivator and a decent form of appreciation. However, the human resources must remember H. Ross Perot's words. "Something in human nature causes us to start slacking off with our moment of greatest accomplishment. As you become successful, you will need a great deal of self-discipline not to lose your sense of balance, humility and commitment."

2. Career Development

"Show me a person who is content with mediocrity and I will show you a person destined for failure"

—Janette Cole

Some employers feel training is a one-time task. Some say their workforce is already skilled and talented so they don't need training and guidance.

But this is not true! Staff need continuous and repetitive development programme to sharpen their knowledge and augment their performance. Encourage your employees to keep learning, unlearning and relearning.

So keep employees updated by subscribing to industry journals, magazines, newsletters, etc. Jim Rohn (America's Foremost Business Philosopher) submitted an article on *www.kaire.com* where he said that one must either modify one's dreams or magnify one's skills. All employees must be aware of the possible budding prospects for them in the future. Don't allow employees to waste their time and energy in any unproductive and non-rewarding task. Utilize them effectively.

Occasionally, organize in-house seminars. It helps employees to update their knowledge, upgrade their information about the latest facts, figures, data and happenings in the industry. In addition to this, the speaker can also share anecdotes, professional stories of success and failure, which is very motivating for the employees.

3. Work Environment and Surrounding

"A nation is held together by shared beliefs and shared attitudes. That is what enables them to rise above the conflicts that plague any society. That is what gives a nation its tone, its fiber, its integrity, its moral style, its capacity to endure"

—John Gardener

A manager needs to generate and preserve an atmosphere where the organizational objectives are clubbed with employees' personal vision and goal. For this, the management must be well-acquainted with the employees' expectations. Also, the employee should be aware of the values and philosophies of his organization. According to Chris Edgelow (Founder and President of Sundance Consulting), "It certainly sound simple enough just tell people what you want them to do so they can get on with the work. Unfortunately, all too often people are told to get on without knowing what is expected of them. They come out of large group announcements wondering what any of this has to do with them". Employees expect decent, truthful, sincere and frank behaviour from you. You are their inspiration, leader, counselor, role model, protector, friend and teacher.

Proper furniture, chairs, desks, air-conditiones, ventilators, computer, file space, fire drills, safety standards, light, stationary, first aid are a few necessities to create a friendly and pleasant work environment. The employees must be treated with attentiveness, diligence and delicacy, since the employees expect wisdom, maturity and fairness from the management. A congenial work environment allows people to be what they are and contribute in their own way.

4. Additional Responsibility

"Far and away the best prize that life offers is the chance to work hard at something worth doing"

—Theodore Roosevelt

Identify employees who are pleading for extra accountable and challenging jobs. Based on their strengths and weaknesses, assign them their desired task. For some employees, extra duty is a sign of trust, reliability and faith.

Some employees will always raise their standards to every challenge and opportunity because they feel that there is always a bigger opportunity waiting for them.

The more challenging task you give them, the better response you get from them. Also, remember the 80:20 principle. 80 per cent of rewards come from 20 per cent of efforts. Hence, focus on 20 per cent of the most important task and avoid the rest. Michael Heppell in his book "*How to be Brilliant*" stated that brilliance is a standard and not a skill. But remember that an additional target or responsibility can be exciting, energetic, vibrant, forceful, innovative, risky, challenging but realistic and achievable. I always believe on "Efforts=Rewards" principle. If rewards are equal or greater than efforts the employees will be positively motivated.

However, with every additional responsibility, employees must have clear information on the chain of command, span of control, mission, vision, values of the company, and the duties and responsibilities with the available power and resources. Only then, the efforts become more rewarding, pleasing, gratifying, meaningful and satisfying.

5. Mutual Trust, Respect and Understanding

> ***"It is amazing how much you can accomplish if you don't care who gets the credit"***
>
> *—Harry Truman*

Treat your employees with respect, admiration and value their self-esteem. Employees are motivated when they feel secured, protected, safe, sound, appreciated, treasured, cherished and respected.

This will directly improve their devotion and faithfulness. An organization can have the best equipment, machinery and tools yet. Human Resources is their most valuable tool.

Hence, it is vital to build your team, trust them, and delegate the task as much as you can. Fight till death for what you and your team really believe in. A successful manager must use more of a "we" and "us" rather than "I" and "Me". A demotivated manager spreads negativity which may lead to office politics.

Mutual trust leads to:

- Congenial work environment
- Optimistic attitude
- Self-respect
- Self-confidence
- Assertiveness among workforce
- Trust is the fundamental pillar of all relationship.

6. Employee Participation

"Bring me solutions, not problems"

—Margaret Thatcher

Employees are motivated when they have the necessary freedom and liberty to perform their task and express their valuable comments, response, opinions, views and advices. It makes them believe that their ideas are listened to and appriciated. Thus, they have a feeling of being a part of the team which builds a congenial employee-employer relation. As the old phrase says, "Birds of a feather flock together."

Take constant inputs from employees, analyze them, evaluate them and if suitable, include them in the organization's overall strategy. Be a very good listener. However, listening means hearing, understanding and interpreting what is said by the employee and then making suitable decision and conclusion.

Your staff members are the ones who are in contact with your customers, dealers, suppliers, retailers, and distributors. They are the ones who know your product, your pricing and your overall marketing strategy, your financial position and the overall business scenario. So, listen to their ideas, opinions, and suggestions, analyze their views, filter them, and then take your own decision based on your experience, expertise, knowledge and gut-feeling. Show empathy towards staff and try to understand their perception as well.

7. Independence/ Autonomy

"To think is easy. To act is difficult. To act as one thinks is the most difficult"

—Johann Wolfgang Von Goethe

All employees have different task to perform in an organization to achieve the organizational goal. They have something different to contribute. Their attitude, behaviour and personalities are unique.

Manager must show consideration for each employee and accept their differences and give them necessary autonomy to perform their task, because for some employees, there is little commitment, enjoyment and pleasure at the workplace without independence. Such recruits will never be valuable assets to their organization.

Set realistic and achievable target for staff by analyzing the strengths, weaknesses and capability of each recruit, i.e., identify the opportunity (be open and flexible), evaluate them, analyze them based on SWOT and then give them the desired independence to perform the task.

As Lee Iacocca believed, "I have found that being honest is the right technique I can use. Right up front, tell people what you're trying to accomplish and what you are willing to sacrifice to accomplish it".

The biggest role of a manager is to pass on the knowledge, duties with appropriate independence to the budding executive. Give them the autonomy to take a stand for what they believe is right. Give them the targets with a desired deadline to achieve meaningful target.

8. Paid Time-off

> ***"Do you reward how long an employee sits in the saddle, or how far s/he rode the horse? Sometimes management seems to reward those who put in long hours at work without looking at the results they accomplish"***
>
> *—Anonymous*

The management can give a day off to employees who produce the maximum sales in a month, or suggest the most creative idea, or conduct the most successful training programme, or give the best cost cutting suggestions or even in recognition of their excellent customer/client service.

Tryon Edwards once said that to waken interest and kindle enthusiasm is the sure way to teach easily and successfully. Paid Time Off (PTO) is the recent strategy a company adopts to retain their existing employees. They offer much needed breaks once a while in the form of personal leaves, sick leaves, vacations or holidays and pays them so that the employees can deal with non-work related issues without a specific reason.

However, before designing an effective programme, the management should establish a clear strategy, guiding principle, procedure and suitable course of action to suit the organizational culture and policy. It can also vary by designation, tenure of service and work experience of the employee.

9. Job Security

> ***"Job Security is gone. The driving force of a career must come from the individual"***
>
> *—Homa Bahrami*

Do you agree with his statement? I do not. In fact, providing job security in an insecure world is a prime motivator. During recession, job security has become extremly significant and important. It's an intangible asset for the employee as it brings consistency, stability, steadiness, firmness in a recruit's career. It also brings dedication, loyalty and commitment towards his responsibilities in the company.

A secure job with a precise combination of financial and non-financial rewards brings financial and mental stability to the staff and reduces employee's attrition. Jack Welch said that, "Strong managers who make tough decisions to cut jobs provide the only true job security in today's world. Weak managers destroy jobs". This will reduce organization's cost of recruitment, induction and training and creates a "win-win" situation for both the employees as well as the employers. With a secured job, employees always feel that you are always there if they need any help, assistance, support and guidance.

Have the courage, vision, game plan for long run and strategies to achieve the goal for yourself and your employees. Never build yourself by damaging others. Dependability, reliability and predictability are the foundation stone for success.

10. Interesting and Exciting Work

> ***"Your goals need to be realistic and achievable. If you set yourself unrealistic goals, you are only setting yourself up for the possibility of failure and disappointment. Larger tasks should be broken down into smaller, more manageable ones. This will make the larger projects seem less daunting. It will also give you a sense of achievement on completion. When calculating how long you will need to complete a task, leave extra time in case the work takes longer than expected. This will relieve the time pressure"***
>
> *—Barbara Nance*

In an ideal work environment, industry, department or team, some employees are devoted, keen, enthusiastic, committed and energized; while some are demotivated, bored and uncommitted. It is the responsibility of the manager to understand employee's welfare, interest, benefits and happiness.

Since the same factor that demotivates some employees, motivates others. For e.g., many employees want demanding and challenging jobs to increase their efficiency and productivity and to break the monotony. Providing such employees better opportunities is the duty of the manager. Be proactive, have a forward-moving game plan, keep a short and long run target (keep updating or modifying your plans) and never stagnate. As Earl Nightingale rightly believed, "Success is the progressive realization of a worthy goal".

"Interesting" and "exciting" work are the two critical combinations for winning and it differentiates ordinary managers from extra ordinary one. Know the current trends and recent development in your industry. Adapt to changes quickly but tactfully, because taking some unusual risk often require courage, keenness, zeal, zest, exhilaration and faith in oneself. Prepare yourself for crisis, panic and emergency situation.

11. Allowing Mistakes

"Trifles make perfection and perfection is no trifle"

—Michelangelo

Understand the fact that most of the staff members are good, but there is always a scope for improvement. And for continuous improvements, mistakes are inevitable. After every mistake, ask your employees what they learned from this?

If the response is positive, you have succeeded to turn a stumbling block into a stepping stone. A reactive or a pessimist manager may hide, cover, neglect or forget his employee's mistakes. But an optimist manager won't do that. They keep learning from every mistake. Failures will never accept their mistake. They ignore them and keep on repeating them again and again. Trust Josh Billings words from his book *Josh Billings: His Sayings* (1869), "Success does not consist in never making blunders, but in never making the same one a second time".

Allowing employees to make mistakes isn't easy, but essential, since you are the "karta", "the head" of the family. Mistakes teach us what should and shouldn't be done at work-place. But after every mistake ask yourself:

- ✓ What was the reason?
- ✓ What can I learn from this?
- ✓ What can be done in the future to avoid such situation again?

Never think you know everything. In fact, believe in the fact that you have most to learn.

12. Be Enthusiastic

"I consider my ability to arouse enthusiasm amongst the men the greatest asset I possess, and the way to develop the best in a man is by appreciation and encouragement"

—Charles Schwab

To have a motivated workforce, the manager must be highly inspiring and encouraging. Enthusiasm is transmissible and communicable from the senior to junior. You have to be dependable, honest, consistent and aggressive; abstemious and reliable — yet enthusiastic. Be passionate about your work.

A confident manager always has high expectations of himself and others. He is pleasing, inspiring, energizing and contributing person. He believes in Ella Wheeler Wilcox quote that :

Rejoice, and men will seek you;
Grieve, and they turn and go;
They want full measure of all your pleasure,
But they do not need your woe.
Be glad, and your friends are many;
Be sad, and you lose them all—
There are none to decline your nectared wine,
But alone you must drink life's gall.

To motivate others, you must first feel positively motivated from within. Every organization has times, when they suffer losses, get entangled in various problems (like union strike, director's resignation, labour issues, etc), which leads to doubt, disappointment and mistrust among employees. It is managers task to rebuild their enthusiasm and restore their faith, commitment and make them feel secure.

Keep yourself constructively occupied to make optimum utilization of available opportunities. Have appealing, pleasing, co-operative and charismatic personality.

13. Be Polite, Honest, Humble and Kind

"The miracle is not to fly in the air, or to walk on water; but to walk on earth"

—Chinese Proverb

Be polite, patient, humble, caring, cheerful and helpful. Recognize your employee's weaknesses, but focus on their strengths. Never compromise on your key values and integrity, since there is no shortcut to success. Make honesty the foundation upon which all other factors will be dependent. Integrity is priceless and can't be purchased by any monetary reward.

Give employees confidence, support and facilitate them to grow and develop. Warren Bennis in his bestselling book "Managing the Dream," mentioned that many leaders do not have empathy, but it is observed that those who lack empathy lack the ability to move people. Leaders who can instill an atmosphere of working together gain respect, taking charge without taking control.

What you say should be simple, clear and easy to understand. Publicly appreciate employees, privately criticize them. An organization can have the best of the equipment, machinery and tools but still man power is their most valuable asset. So share your knowledge, skills and expertise with your people and guide your employees.

Never see them as a threat. Always be predictable in any unpredictable situation. Be friendly with your staff, but not too personal. Always maintain a distance and dignity with employees.

Finally, let politeness take the driver's seat, since it leads to self-esteem and self-worth. On the other hand, rudeness is like a wild plant. It obstructs the most talented, capable, clever and gifted minds.

14. Give and Receive Honest Feedback

> ***"Don't flatter yourself that friendship authorizes you to say disagreeable things to your intimates. The nearer you come into relation with a person, the more necessary do tact and courtesy become"***
>
> *—Oliver Wendell Holmes*

Giving regular feedback to employees helps them understand their strengths, weaknesses, problems and areas where they need improvement. Always speak the truth. Periodically, employees expect honest feedback from their bosses.

They should know what is expected from them and what they are actually doing. If the outcome is positive, they must be rewarded. If not, the manager must properly mentor them and guide them about how to perform, where and why they are lacking, and even their positive factors.

Keep an open door feedback policy. Accept and learn from criticism and constantly give and ask for opinions to enhance your performance. Be open to receive positive criticism, new ideas, opportunities and threats.

However, avoid arguments on unimportant matters. Recognize the non-verbal signs like eye-contact, gestures, facial expressions, postures, body language, etc. Never fear rejections. Give straight, genuine, frank, earnest, specific and on-the-spot feedback.

15. Encourage Loyalty and Team Spirit

> ***"The man who does not work for the love of work but only for money is likely neither to make money nor find much fun in life"***
>
> *—Charles M. Schwab*

In the corporate world, there is no magic wand to build team spirit and loyalty among workers. It is the result of sincere efforts and dedication. Don't bad mouth or back-bite your peers, bosses, subordinates, colleagues or juniors.

> ***"If you're in a meeting and someone is playing politics, just tell them; you're playing politics, come back when you feel better"***
>
> *—Sir John Harvey Jones*

When things go wrong, and they sometimes will, don't stag-off, complain, pass unjustified comments or criticize your team for the failures.

You are equally guilty of their mistakes and errors. Accept that it was a cohesive effort, learn from it and move on.

If your employees are right, be bold, open, and honest. Be their mentor, protector, defender to support them and guide them. Look for positive things in every employee, treat them equally with decency, respect and be proud of them. It is cheaper to retain and keep motivating an existing employee than to recruit and train a new one.

Focus on the positive side, things you have, rather than merely complaining about things we don't have. Believe in personal and organizational values, integrity and character. Never make excuses for personal failures.

16. Reward Innovative Ideas

> ***"Small people talk about other people, mediocre people talk about things, great people talk about ideas"***
>
> *—Anonymous*

In modern business world, past glory and achievements are insignificant. We have to live in present, continuously perform, deliver and innovate.

Encourage the staff to contribute innovative ideas. For this, it is vital to create an environment where every employee shares their ideas and innovative thoughts. Managers must identify employees who have crab attitude, i.e. employees who are jealous and pull others down when they give some innovative idea or suggestion.

Bernie Milano (President and a trustee of the KPMG Foundation the KPMG Disaster Relief Fund) said that the greatest advancement of this century — the light bulb, airplane and computer, were created by innovators — people who imagine things that did not exist and asked why.

Being an outstanding employee requires a touch of this inventor's spirit, a determination to persistently strive to create value.

Be an active listener by:

- Paying attention to innovative ideas.
- Asking relevant questions to show interest.

Inculcate the burning desire and self-discipline among employees to constantly learn new things and suggest innovative ideas.

17. Have Fun and Enjoy Yourself

"Most people go to their graves with music still in them"

—Oliver Holmes

The following are the advantages if you enjoy yourself at the work-place:

- You can work without supervision
- You are always on time
- You foster loyalty, mutual trust, growth and development
- You encourage the team members
- You are reliable in testing times
- You never envy your co-workers, colleagues and juniors
- You think beyond what is achievable and possible.

All these traits make your personality:

- Confident
- Co-operative
- Considerate
- Cheerful
- Courteous.

A successful manager identifies his area of specialization, domain and competences based on his limitation and strengths. He believes in the idea of delegating authority and power to perform the task. He avoids daily, routine, regular tasks and concentrates on unusual interesting activity.

Marc Hempel and Neil Gaiman in their book *"The Sandman – the kindly ones"* (9th collection of issues in the DC Comics series) mentioned that it has always been the prerogative of children and half-wits to point out that the emperor has no clothes. But the half-wit remains a half-wit and the emperor remains an emperor. An unsuccessful, pessimist manager will always envy you. In a crisis situation, remain cool, calm, and in control. Never brag about your successes and achievements. Develop a sense of humor. It makes difficult problems manageable.

18. Relieve Employees when they are Stressed

> ***"Many managers follow the notion of busy fools and confuse hard work with long hours. They think because they work 15 hour days and forget their children's names, they must be bloody good managers. The best sales manager I worked with never worked beyond 5.30 p.m"***
>
> *—Caspian Woods*

Both the employee and employer must understand that pain and pleasure are part of work. Some days will be boring, frustrating, disappointing, idle and dull while some will be demanding, challenging, exciting and busy. Laid back attitude, hurry, irritation, frustration, boredom, inappropriate behaviour, disappointments are some common symptoms of stress.

An employee may appear as motivated from outside, but can be totally hollow from within. There is no task worth doing that deteriorates or affects the health of the employee. As Thomas Edison once rightly said, "Opportunity is missed by most people because it comes dressed in overalls and looks like work". When any human is stressed you must find out the following:

- Why is the employee stressed?
- What are the reasons?
- When is he stressed from?
- How can I de-stress him?
- Whom to be blamed for such problem?
- What should be done to avoid such situation again?

If employees are stressed, they need a break from their routine schedule. Excitement job, job enrichment, or even a transfer in different department/ branch can have a positive reinforcement. It shows consideration, courtesy, politeness and thoughtfulness towards employees and raises their morale and productivity.

19. Foster a "Forgive and Forget" Approach

"Forgive the other person but don't forget their name"

—John Kennedy

Inculcate the habit of forgiving employees' small mistakes. Don't hold guilt or grudges for too long. When someone admits and apologizes for his mistake, try to forgive him. This will improve mutual trust, integrity and build a long-term relationship.

Encouraging people to forgive others begins with inspiring yourself. Never indulge in politics and don't allow your employees to do that as well. Be considerate and kind about their problems. Treating employees with courtesy and kindness as they are the hallmarks of a generous manager.

Forgiveness must be genuine and real; try to practice it on daily basis. You and your team can never work together efficiently if you hold grudges for too long. So, to create good work environments promote the attitude of forgiving your employees minor errors and mistakes.

However, it doesn't mean getting cheated again and again. As a popular saying goes, "If you cheat me once, shame on you; if you cheat me twice, shame on me". People who don't learn from their past mistakes are fools. Never allow employees to win by any unethical/ dishonest way as it always provides a short term/ temporary success, but is immaterialist in long run. Encourage employees to win competitively and graciously, as it gives immense satisfaction and pride.

20. Fear Motivation

Finally, let me share an anecdote with you. Mr. "X" started his own small scale business and appointed "Y" to look after the sales. Initially, "Y" worked with zeal and enthusiasm and achieved his targets before the deadline. But after a few months, he struggled to meet his monthly quota and started losing interest. Mr. "X" encouraged him, and tried to motivate him by several monetary and non-monetary ways. But nothing changed after a month. Finally, Mr. "X" called Mr. "Y" into his office and said, "If you don't perform, you are fired the next month". Like a charm, his efficiency and dedication saw a boost within a month.

In this case, **fear** is the biggest motivation for Mr. "Y". We will find such people in all organization. Hence, you must adopt "pull and push" based motivational strategy; i.e., – "carrot and stick approach". "Carrot/ pull" technique is by offering financial and non-financial rewards; whereas "stick/ push" technique is a fear motivation to keep people moving with a stick from behind.

It can be fear of disgrace, embarrassment, dishonour, humiliation, indignity, infamy, ignominy, discomfiture, awkwardness, shame or mortification among peers, bosses or colleagues. Fear of removal, transfer, demotion or criticism can be a good motivator in short run. However, it can sometime lead to high stress level and create an unpleasant negative environment.

In such case, employees look for security rather than an opportunity. But, it helps to utilize 100 per cent of employees' talent, ability and potential. It builds the necessary self-confidence and the employees stop the habit of procrastination.

Promise Yourself

Promise yourself to be so strong that nothing can disturb your peace of mind.
To talk health, happiness, and prosperity to every person you meet.
To make all your friends feel like there is something in them.
To look at the sunny side of everything and make your optimism come true.
To think only of the best, to work only for the best, and expect only the best.
To be just as enthusiastic about the success of others as you are about your own.
To forget the mistakes of the past and press on the greater achievements of the future.
To wear a cheerful countenance at all times and give every living person you meet a smile.
To give so much time to the improvement of yourself that you have no time to criticize others.
To be too large for worry, too noble for anger, and too strong for fear, and too happy to permit the presence of trouble.

—The Optimist Creed

14. Motivate Your Ordinary Performers... Convert them into Extraordinary Ones...

Mr. Prakash, a senior business executive in a mid-sized business unit, had been on the job for seven years. His performance was average, but, the other employees who had been in the organization for less than four years were as competent as Mr. Prakash. Inspite of that the company didn't want to lose an honest and sincere employee. So, his boss started analyzing the reasons for his average and ordinary performance.

Employees like Mr. Prakash exist in all organizations and the challenge for their bosses is to convert such ordinary performers into extraordinary ones. But the question is how and why?

The reasons for ordinary performance can be many. Inability to accept challenging task, fear of failure, lack of purpose/direction/vision/confidence, communication barrier, etc. Signs indicating an employee is dissatisfied are: sluggishness, slowness, lack of interest/concern, boredom, droopiness, inaccuracy, mistakes, miscalculations, absenteeism etc. In a nutshell, an average or below average performance is an indicator of dissatisfaction.

They use statements like "we don't get any credit for our work", "I will not deliver my 100 per cent", "We don't get any extra money for additional task", "Change is difficult", etc.

Converting your ordinary worker to an extraordinary one can be a demanding, taxing and difficult job — yet, it can be done with an ease. This is because a loyal and dedicated employee is predictable in any unfavorable and difficult situation; through all thick and thin of the organization.

A positively motivated employee can work without supervision, easily accept change, and knows exactly what is expected from him and how he should deliver. He ensures that he always meets his targets and deadlines. However, everyone expects some rewards (monetary/non-monetary) for their contribution in the organization.

However, such expectations may differ based on their designation, work-experience, educational qualification, etc. Maslow's Need Hierarchy

Theory stated that in addition, to financial gains, an employee or any individual has social needs, self-esteem needs, autonomy needs, and self-actualization needs.

Any employee who is content and happy in his workplace performs his task efficiently. Each worker, unlike other aspects of production (e.g., machine, money, method, material and market), is unique in the way he thinks, believes, perceives, distinguishes, observes, analysis, examines, inspects and scrutinizes. Hence, it is vital to understand the motivations of each employee. Motivation encourages employees to work with passion, enthusiasm, interest, eagerness and without pressure, strain, anxiety and tension.

Twyla Dell, in *An Honest Day's Work,* wrote that the heart of motivation is to give people what they really want most from work. The more you are able to provide what they want, the more you should expect what you really want, namely: productivity, quality and service. Motivation need not always be classy, noble, costly or pricey.

45 Quick Tips to Motivate Demotivated Employees

Here are 45 ways to motivate demotivated employees:

1. Involve your team emotionally, mentally and physically in any task.
2. Accept individual differences and adopt a unique management style for each team member.
3. Know their strengths, weaknesses, capabilities, talent and focus on their positives to eliminate their negatives.
4. Set difficult but realistic and measurable targets with the desired deadlines.
5. Allow them to make mistakes and learn from them.
6. Ensure that they learn from their past mistakes and never repeat them again.
7. Give them best resources, if you expect best optimal results.
8. Train them to prioritize their task and fill their time effectively and efficiently.
9. Maintain an open door regular feedback and suggestion policy on their performance, because without regular feedback, employees become irritated, disturbed, upset, annoyed, discouraged and pessimistic about their efforts in the organization.
10. Never bank too much on luck. Luck is the meeting point between efforts and rewards.

11. Tell them that fortune favours those who believe in smart work with the required discipline and devotion.
12. Teach them to take their own decisions based on their experience, expertise, knowledge and institution.
13. Inspire them to be creative and innovative.
14. Teach them to distinguish between honest and dishonest criticism.
15. Tell them that never to be disheartened, discouraged or disappointed by failures.
16. Teach them to carefully choose their words and think before, and not after, they speak.
17. Avoid holding grudges for too long. Inculcate a "forgive and forget" approach.
18. Teach them never to compromise on key values, principles and integrity as these are the pillars for success.
19. Give and receive sincere and specific compliments.
20. Repeatedly remind them of the story of hare and tortoise. Over-confidence is dangerous.
21. Don't rush to any conclusions.
22. Give the right job to the right man and ensure that the right man is on the right job.
23. Celebrate their success and achievements.
24. Create a congenial work environment.
25. Inspire mutual trust, loyalty, respect, understanding and team spirit.
26. Appreciate their valuable contribution and make them proud of their work.
27. Don't encourage employees to bad-mouth or slag-off other employees, or play internal politics.
28. Encourage collective goal setting and team work, as it improves their quality, productivity and efficiency.
29. Teach them to convert their assurance into commitment.
30. You set an example and train them to work really, really hard.
31. Teach them to be prepared for ups and downs, joys, sorrows and success and failures.
32. Persuade them to be optimistic and have a positive attitude.

33. Suggest to stay away from employees who have a pessimistic, attitude and are zealous, fervent and obsessive.

34. Inspire them to play to win by inculcating a strong burning desire to be the victor.

35. Enthusiasm is free and contagious. So spread it.

36. Continuously break the emotional and mental blockage of the employees.

37. Train them to consistently prepare themselves and deliver, since, in modern business, past success and achievement doesn't count much.

38. Decide and prepare a long-term and short-term game plan.

39. Train them to consistently prepare themselves and deliver; as in modern business past success and achievement doesn't count much.

40. Keep your spirit and confidence high in any unfavourable environment or situation.

41. Have one-on-one meeting with each employee to understand their motivational factors.

42. Ask them about their career goals, ambitions, objectives, aspirations and targets.

43. Give them an opportunity to express their views, opinions, suggestions and give their valuable feedback. This gives them an opportunity to prove their intelligence and believe that they are the part of the team.

44. Emphasize and suggest them to build a long-term relationship with their customers, clients, suppliers, buyers, dealers and shareholders.

45. Finally help them make a chart to combine organization's and individual's performance. The chart should help:

    a. Identify your goals based on organization's vision, mission and policy.

    b. Identify the employees to achieve their targets based on their strengths/weaknesses/ability and capability.

    c. Give them the required authority and power to perform their duties and responsibilities.

    d. Regularly monitor whether the goals are being met or not.

e. If YES, Reward them for their performance and return to Step a.

f. If NO, Give them proper feedback and take corrective actions (return to Step d).

My Comfort Zone

I used to have a comfort zone where I knew I wouldn't fail.
The same four walls and busywork were really more like jail.
I longed so much to do the things I'd never done before,
But stayed inside my comfort zone and paced the same old floor.
I said it didn't matter that I wasn't doing much.
I said I didn't care for things like commission checks and such.
I claimed to be so busy with the things inside the zone,
But deep inside I longed for something special of my own.
I couldn't let my life go by just by watching others win.
I held my breath; I stepped outside and let the change begin.
I took a step and with new strength I'd never felt before,
I kissed my comfort zone goodbye and closed and locked the door.
If you're in a comfort zone, afraid to venture out,
Remember that all winners were at one time filled with doubt.
A step or two and words of praise can make your dreams come true.
Reach for your future with a smile; success is there for you!

—Unknown

5 Golden Rules to Manage Time

Time management is a crucial tool for success. John Rohn, the world's leading motivational speaker, philosopher and entrepreneur once said, "I find it fascinating that most people plan their vacations with better care than they plan their lives. Perhaps that is because escape is easier than change."

We often complain that we have a short life and there are plenty of things to be done with very limited time at hand. We shall be saved from regret, stress, tension, humiliation and will make all round progress in our personal and academic life, if we realize the value and importance of time management.

Time management is extremely crucial for employees. Infact time management is a skill, for every employee here are five golden rules:

1. Procrastination Steals Time

As James Debary rightly said, "He slept beneath the moon, He slept beneath the sun, He lived the life of going to do and died with nothing done." When a work is delayed, the time which would have been profitably used is wasted. Time wasted is time lost forever.

It can neither be retrieved, nor stored for later use. Remember the old saying, "Time and Tide waits for no one." Beating procrastination helps you quickly eliminate the most common time-waster. Never leave till tomorrow what you can do today. A good plan executed now is better than a perfect plan next week.

2. Prioritize Your Task

Pareto's principle or the "80:20" rule says that typically 80 per cent of the unfocussed efforts generate only 20 per cent of results. The remaining 80 per cent of results are achieved with 20 per cent of the efforts.

Maintain a "to-do-list" which helps you to focus on the most important priorities and a "daily/weekly/long time planner" which indicates how to really spend your time and effective scheduling of your personal/short/long-term goals. In brief, plan efficiently to make use of your time by concentrating on results, not on being busy.

3. Have a Contingency Plan

Have a Plan B and Plan C to avoid disasters. Always expect the unexpected. When things go wrong be ready to overcome it. Say you are studying for your exams and there is a power failure, you must plan beforehand what to do? As Henry Ford said, "People who have no time don't think. The more you think, the more you have time."

Evaluate how you are spending your time and how can you make better use of time by combining several activities like reading while commuting. Start by doing what is necessary then what is possible and suddenly you are doing the impossible.

4. Learn to say "NO"

Say "No" to non-essential tasks. Cut out the job not required, and dedicate your time to your goals and schedules before agreeing to take on additional work. Take a break when needed and be motivated, dedicated and focused to meet your deadlines. "Many managers follow the notion of busy fools and confuse hard work with long hours. They think because they work 15 hour days and forget their children's names, they must be bloody good managers. The best manager I worked with never worked beyond 5.30pm." — Caspian Woods (from Acorns – *"How to build your brilliant business from Scratch"*).

5. Health is Wealth

Manage your health, get plenty of sleep and exercise, food which improves focus and concentration. A healthy mind dwells in a healthy body.

Stay ahead of the stress game. Michael Miller MD, Centre for Preventive Cardiology feels that the recommendations for a healthy living are exercise, eating healthy and having a laugh few times a day. Health management is very important if you want a balanced life-style.

Proper healthcare results in lesser number of sick leaves, higher levels of active performance at work, which in turn leads to faster completion, lesser time wasted in breaks due to physical strain, and many such time saving benefits.

Always remember it is easier to find something to do with extra time than to find extra time to do something.

My Wage

I bargained with life for a penny, and life would pay no more,
However I begged at evening; When I counted my scanty store;
For life is a just an employer, He gives you what you ask,
But once you have set the wages, Why, you must bear the task.
I worked for a mennial's hire, only to learn dismayed,
That any wage I had asked of life, life would have paid.

—Jessie B. Rittenhouse

Leadership and Motivation

If no one is following, you are not leading. A good leader constantly motivates his work force. There is a direct relationship between a good leader and a positively motivated work-force.

Faye Wattleton said, "The only safe ship in a storm is leadership." Leadership involves influencing a group of people to move towards setting a goal or goal achievement. A leader influences people by providing purpose, direction and motivation while operating to accomplish the mission and improving the organization. A good leader leads, but doesn't push.

There are different types of leadership styles. They are *Laissez Faire*, bureaucratic, charismatic, autocratic, democratic, people oriented, task-oriented, a servant leader, transactional leader, transformational leader, environment leader and situational leader.

However, leaders are different from managers. All managers are not leaders. In 1977, Abraham Zaleznik mentioned the differences between a leader and a manager, which are as follows:

- Manager administers, leader innovates.
- Manager asks how and when, leader asks what and why.
- Manager focuses on system, leader focuses on people.
- Manager does the things right, leader does the right things.
- Manager maintains, leader develops.
- Manager relies on control, leader inspires trust.
- Manager has a short-term perspective; leader has a long-term perspective.

- Manager accepts the status quo, leader challenges the status quo.
- Manager has an eye on the bottom line; leader has an eye on the horizon.
- Manager initiates, leader originates.
- Managers emulate the classic good soldiers, leaders are their own person.
- Managers copy, leaders displays originality.

Thus, leadership differs, in that, it makes followers want to achieve high goals, rather than simply bossing around people. "Inventories can be managed, but people must be led"

—H. Ross Perot

Clear vision, consistency, self-sacrifice, confidence, persistence, initiate, innovation, planning, risk-bearing, time management, decision making, charisma, timeliness, passion, enthusiasm, technical proficiency, emotional maturity, flexibility, rational thinking, motivation and honesty are the suggested qualities in a leader.

The key to successful leadership today is influence, not authority.

—Kenneth Blanchard

A leader need to understand an employee by analyzing his strengths/weaknesses, character, knowledge, skills and continuously seeks self-improvement for setting an example. When things go wrong, he takes responsibility of the action.

He knows his employees well, keeps them informed. He develops a sense of responsibility among them and effectively communicates the task to them. He motivates them, inspires a shared vision, ensures that the task is understood and accomplished by training/counseling them as a team, thus enabling and encouraging others to act and ensuring fullest utilization of available resources.

A leader sets realistic and attainable goal by developing a programme to achieve each goal and involving all his subordinates in the goal setting process, keeping in mind that he can't please everyone. James Shore believed that some of the most talented people are terrible leaders because they have a crippling need to be loved by everyone. Tony Blair also added by saying that the art of leadership is saying "no", not "yes", it is very easy to say "yes".

The leader should lead by example, as he is a father figure. "The leaders who work most effectively, it seems to me, never say "I". And that's not because they have trained themselves not to say "I". They don't think "I". They think "We", they think "Team". They understand their job is to make the team function. They accept responsibility and don't sidestep it, but "we" gets the credit. That is what creates trust, what enables you to get the task done."

—Peter Drucker

Before You

Before you speak, listen.
Before you write, think.
Before you spend, earn.
Before you invest, investigate.
Before you criticize, wait.
Before you pray, forgive.
Before you quit, try.
Before you retire, save.
Before you die, give.

—William Arthur Ward

Lives of Ten Indian Business Magnets

Here is a brief life history of ten Indian business tycoons whose lives gives us great motivation to move ahead.

1. Dhirubhai Ambani – The Unforgettable

"Between my past, the present and the future, there is one common factor: Relationship and Trust. This is the foundation of our growth". This memorable line having a significant meaning was said by a great Indian Entrepreneur and Industrialist – Dhirubhai Ambani.

Dhirajlal Hirachand Ambani (popularly known as Dhirubhai Ambani) was born on 28th December, 1932, at Chorwad, Gujarat. He married Kokilaben and had two son, Mukesh and Anil Ambani and two daughters, Nita Kothari and Deepti Salgaocar.

He started his career with A. Besse and Company at the age of 16, for a salary of Rs.300/-. He returned to India in 1962 and with a capital investment of Rs. 1500, he started Reliance Commercial Corporation. The primary business was to import polyester and export spices. Later in 1966, he started his first textile mill (manufactured by polyester fiber yarns) at Naroda, Ahmedabad which was branded as "Vimal". In India, he pioneered the idea of **equity shares** and in 1977, more than 58,000 investors from various parts of the country invested in Reliance Initial Public Offer (IPO). His philosophy of life was, "Our dreams have to be bigger. Our ambitions higher. Our commitment deeper. Our efforts greater. This is my dream for Reliance and for India". He diversified his business in to Information Technology, energy, power, telecommunication, infrastructure, capital market and logistics. He once said, "think big, think fast, think ahead. Ideas are no one's monopoly". Dhirubhai's bitter rivals were Nusli Wadia of Bombay Dyeing, Ramanath Goenka of Indian Express, and Vishwanath Pratap Singh – former Prime Minister of India.

He died on 6 July, 2002 from brain stroke. After his death, former Prime Minister Atal Bihari Vajpayee said that the country has lost an iconic proof of what an ordinary Indian, fired by the spirit of enterprise and drive by determination achieved in his own lifetime. During his time, Reliance had an annual gross turnover of around Rs. 75,000 crores. On his first death anniversary, the Union Government released a postage stamp in his memory.

Some of his achievements are:

- In June 1998, he was awarded "Dean Medal" by the Wharton school, University of Pennsylvania for setting an example of leadership.
- In November 2000, he was awarded "Man of the Century" by Chemtech Foundation and Chemical Engineering.
- In 2000, he featured among "The 50 most Powerful Asians" by Asiaweek magazine.
- In August 2001, he received the "Lifetime Achievement Award" by The Economic Times.

2. Mukesh D. Ambani

Mukesh Ambani (born on 19 April, 1957, in Yemen) is the Chairman, Managing Director and the largest shareholder of Reliance Industries Limited – India's largest private sector company. He is also the Chairman of Reliance Retail Limited, and Director of Reliance Europe Limited and Pratham India Education Initiative.

Mukesh Ambani is the elder son of Late Dhirubhai Ambani, the founder of Reliance Industries. After his father's death, the company was split between the two brothers. His younger brother Anil Ambani heads Anil Dhirubhai Ambani Group.

Mukesh Ambani completed his schooling from St. Xavier's High School in Mumbai. He graduated in Chemical Engineering from University of Mumbai and pursued Masters in Business Administration from Stanford University, but dropped out after first year and joined Reliance in 1981. He is married to Nita Ambani and they have three children – Akash, Isha and Anant. He founded the world's largest grassroots Petroleum Refinery at Jamnagar, Gujarat, India. The refinery has a capacity of 6, 60,000 barrels per day, about 33 million tons per year. He initiated Reliance's backward integration from textiles into polyester fibers and then into petroleum refining, oil and gas exploration and production. He is the founder of Reliance Infocomm Limited, which is now known as Reliance Communication Limited.

He is the richest man in Asia and fifth in the world. He is associated to 167 board members in 7 different organizations across 3 different industries. He also owns the Indian Premium League Team "Mumbai Indians", Dhirubhai Ambani International School, Mumbai, and is currently building the most expensive house in the world.

Some of the honour and awards bestowed on him are mentioned as follows:

- In 2010, he was named among the most powerful people in the world by Forbes in its list of "68 people who matter most".
- He received the US-India Business Council (USIBC) 'Global Vision' 2007 Award for Leadership in 2007.
- He is the only Indian CEO to be a Council Member of WBCSD (World Business Council for Sustainable Development).
- Conferred 'ET Business Leader of the Year' Award by The Economic Times (India) in the year 2006.
- Awarded the Degree Honoris Causa, Honorary Doctorate by the Maharaja Sayajirao University in 2007.
- Received the India Business Leadership Award by CNBC-TV18 in 2007.
- Received the first NDTV Profit 'Global Indian Leader Award' from Hon'ble Prime Minister of India, Shri Manmohan Singh in New Delhi in 2006.
- Had the distinction and honour of being the cochair at the World Economic Forum in Davos, Switzerland.
- Ranked 42nd among the 'World's Most Respected Business Leaders' and second among the four Indian CEOs featured in a survey conducted by Pricewaterhouse Coopers and published in Financial Times, London, in November, 2004.
- Conferred the World Communication Award for the 'Most Influential Person' in Telecommunications by Total Telecom, in October, 2004.
- Conferred the 'Asia Society Leadership Award' by the Asia Society, Washington D.C., USA, in May, 2004.
- He is a member of the Prime Minister's Council on Trade and Industry, Government of India and the Board of Governors of the National Council of Applied Economic Research, New Delhi.
- He is also a member of the Indo-US CEOs Forum, the International Advisory Board of Citigroup, International Advisory Board of the National Board of Kuwait and McKinsey Advisory Council.

- He is the Chairman, Board of Governors of the Indian Institute of Management, Bangalore and a member of the Advisory Council of the Indian Institute of Technology, Mumbai.
- He is a member of the Advisory Council for the Graduate School of Business of the Stanford University.

His vision in life is, "I think that our fundamental belief is that for us growth is a way of life and we have to grow at all times"; 'Always invest in businesses of the future and in talent' is his success mantra. He believes that senior people must give bright 25-year-olds the opportunity to contribute meaningfully.

3. Anil Dhirubhai Ambani

Anil Dhirubhai Ambani – a Bachelor in Science from the University of Bombay (now University of Mumbai) and Masters in Business Administration from the Wharton School at the University of Pennsylvania was born on June 4, 1959. He is the youngest son of Dhirubhai Ambani. He is married to Tina Ambani, and has two sons, Jai Anmol and Jai Anshul. He joined Reliance in 1983 as co-chief executive officer. Prior split in Reliance group, he was Vice-Chairman and Managing Director of Reliance Industries Limited (RIL). After the split, he incorporated Anil Dhirubhai Ambani Group (ADAG), of which he is the Chairman and includes companies like Reliance Communication, Reliance Capital, Reliance Energy, Reliance Natural Resources Ltd. He is a man of courage and conviction.

He believed; "It is hope in this wider sense which enabled my father to build, from scratch, one of India's largest modern enterprises. His was an undertaking powered by hard work, initiative, self-belief but, above all else, the capacity, as he would often say, "to dream with your eyes wide open". He is the President of the Dhirubhai Ambani Institute of Information and Communication Technology, Gandhinagar, and a member of Wharton Board of Overseers, The Wharton School, USA; Board of Governors, Indian Institute of Management (IIM), Ahmedabad; Board of Governors, Indian Institute of Technology (IIT), Kanpur; Executive Board, Indian School of Business (ISB), Hyderabad.

He raised $ 3 billion from the highly anticipated Initial Public Offering of Reliance Power in less than 15 months, which is the biggest in Indian history. Forbes magazine listed him as the 6th richest man in the world after his brother Mukesh Ambani. Since his wealth tripled in only one year in percentage terms, he was the world's fastest-growing multi-billion-dollar individual. His success mantra is, "I think you have to work with people, and when I talk about managing relationships, don't think the derogatory "managed relationships". It is a question of sharing emotion and feelings. The common denominator of everything can't be money, and it should not be money".

Some of his awards and recognitions are as follows:

- Voted the 3rd most powerful person in India in the 2009 India Today Power List.
- "Businessman of the Year 1997" by Business India.
- "MTV Youth Icon of the Year" in September 2003.
- "CEO of the Year 2004" in the Platts Global Energy Awards.
- "The Entrepreneur of the Decade Award" by the Bombay Management Association.
- "Businessman of the Year 2006" by The Times of India.
- "Best Role Model" in the pool conducted by India Today Magazine in August 2006.
- "Leaders of the millennium in Business and Finance" by Asiaweek Magazine.

4. Indra Krishnamurthy Nooyi

Indra Krishnamurthy Nooyi was born on 28 October, 1955 in Chennai, Tamil Nadu, India. She completed her Bachelor's degree in Chemistry from Madras Christian College in 1974; her Post Graduate Diploma in Business Administration from Indian Institute of Management Studies (Calcutta), and her Masters Degree in Management from Yale School of Management. She lives in Greenwich, Connecticut with her husband Raj, a software engineer and two daughters, Pritha and Tara.

Before joining PepsiCo in 1994 as Senior Vice-President of Corporate Strategy and Development, she worked with The Boston Consulting Group (BCG), Motorola and ABB. She was promoted as the Chief Financial Officer (CFO), and later elected as the Chairwoman and Chief Executive Officer (CEO) of PepsiCo on 1 October, 2006, as a successor of Steve Reinemund. She played a prominent role in the acquisition of Tropicana, company's merger with Quaker, and the deal of YUM Brands, the parent company of fast food properties like Taco Bell, Pizza Hut, and KFC. As of date, she is the only Indian woman to become the Chief Executive Officer of the more $25 billion multinational company. She was listed on Wall Street Journal's "50 Women to watch in 2005". Fortune magazine named her No. 1 "Most Powerful Woman in Business" in 2006 and 2007.

According to the polls conducted by Forbes magazine in 2007, she ranked fifth on the list of "the world's 100 most powerful women". In 2007, she was awarded Padma Bhushan by Government of India. Time's listed her among "100 Most Influential People in the world" in 2007 and 2008. She is a member of "Bilderberg group" which is a highly secretive group. She is a member of the Boards of the Lincoln Center for the performing Arts in the New York City. Her success mantra in life is, "there are no limits to what you can do", she added, "Success isn't money, prestige, or power because net-worth can never define self-worth. True success is being happy with yourself, is being fulfilled and that comes from devoting your time, your life, to doing what you love the most". She believes, "What's important is trying to be the best and working to get there. And that's how you fulfill your potential", she elaborated, "Never stop learning. It's a multi-cultural world out there and we all have to interact with people who are different... success comes with reaching out integrating with the community... and giving back to the communities and neighbourhoods, more than what you took out of them. Hence, keep an open mind". Finally she explained that the three critical pillars of success are, "family, friends and faith", she said, "when things look bleak and uncertain, it's your family, friends and faith that pull you through....And when I'm wrestling with change in my life, good or bad, the first place I turn to, is my religion. I tell you, it really helps".

5. Azim Hasham Premji

Azim Hasham Premji, CEO and Chairman of Wipro, one of the largest software companies in India was born on 24 July, 1945; he finished his schooling from St. Mary School, I.C.S.E in Mazgaon, Mumbai and his undergraduate electronic engineering from Stanford University, USA. He is married to Yasmeen Premji; has two children – Rishad and Tariq. He presently lives in Bangalore, India. He joined Wipro at the age of 21, immediately after his father's sudden demise with a vision to build an organization on the foundation of his values. And the rest is a history; he never looked back after that. Forbes rated him as the richest Indian from 1999 to 2005; as of 6 October, 2007 he has wealth worth of $13.6 billion. The total revenue from I.T, BPO and R$D Services accounts to nearly $5 billion and Wipro has a presence in over 50 countries; it was the first Indian Company to embrace Six Sigma, the first Software Services Company in the world to achieve SEI CMM Level 5 and it also became the world's first organization to achieve PCMM Level 5 (People Capability Maturity Model).

His objective in life is, "We believe this combination of excellence in operations and strong execution of our strategy is critical to achieve our vision. We will continue to focus on both in future as well."

His tip on success:

- Have the courage to think big.
- Never compromise on fundamental values, no matter what the situation.
- Build up self-confidence, always look ahead.
- Always have the best around you, even if they are better than you are.
- Have an obsessive commitment to quality.
- Play to win.
- Leave the rest to the force beyond.

Some of his renowned honors and recognitions are as follows:

- In 2011, he has been awarded Padma Vibhushan, the second highest civilian award by the Govt. of India.
- He was awarded "Business Man of the Year 2000" by Business India.
- Forbes rated him as one of ten people globally, who have the most "power to effect change" in March 2003.

- Fortune in August 2003 ranked him as one of the 25 most powerful business leaders outside the US.
- Business Week in October 2003 featured him on their cover with the sobriquet "India's Tech King".
- "Business Leader of the Year 2004" by the Economic Times.
- Financial Times included him in the list of top 25 billionaires in November 2004.
- Time listed him in April 2004 as one amongst 100 most influential people in the world.

Azim Premji had set up the Azim Premji Foundation with a focus to provide financial resources to the weaker section of the society. "It aims at marketing a tangible impact on identified social issues by working in active partnership with the government and other related sectors of society". It focuses on "creating effective and scalable models that significantly improve the quantity of leaning in the school and ensure satisfactory ownership by the community in the management of the school".

6. K. V. Kamat

K.V. Kamat was born on 2 December, 1947. He is currently living in Mumbai and is married. He has a son and a daughter. He completed his schooling from St. Aloysius School, Karnataka; his Bachelor's degree in Mechanical Engineering from National Institute of Technology, Karnataka; and his Master's in Business Administration from Indian Institute of Management, Ahmedabad.

In 1971, he joined ICICI (an Indian financial institution) in the Project Finance Division that later founded ICICI Bank and merged with it in 2001. Before becoming the Chief Executive Office and Managing Director of ICICI Bank, he was in the Asian Development Bank, Manila in 1988 and was involved in various projects in China, India, Indonesia, Philippines, Bangladesh and Vietnam. K.V. Kamat is the Managing Director and Chief Executive Officer of ICICI Bank, which is India's second largest bank. He initiated and implemented ICICI's computerization programmes. Over the years, he diversified the business across banking, insurance, asset management in India and expanded the corporate business by catering the needs of corporate and retail customers.

His honours and recognition are as follows:

- In 2008, he received Padma Bhushan.
- He was awarded "Businessman of the Year" by Forbes Asia.
- The Economic Times conferred him "Business Leader of the Year" in 2007.
- He received Business Standard "Banker of the Year" award.
- In 2006, CNBC-TV18 awarded him "Outstanding Business Leader of the Year."
- He received "Most e-savvy CEO amongst Asian banks" by the Asian Banker Journal of Singapore.
- He was recognised as "Finance Man of the Year award" by the Mumbai Management Association.
- The World HRD Congress rewarded him "Best CEO for Innovative HR practices".
- He conferred Business India's "Businessman of the Year" award in 2005.
- He was recognised by CNBC as "Asian Business Leader of the Year" in 2001.
- The Banaras Hindu University conferred him with an honorary PhD.

Mr. Kamath is a member of the governing board on various educational institutions including Indian Institute of Management (IIM) – Ahmedabad, Indian School of Business (ISB), National Institute of Bank Management and Manipal Academy of Higher Education.

He is a member of the National Council of Confederation of Indian Industry (CII). His success mantra in life is, "When your back is against the wall, you think beyond your normal boundaries."

7. Lakshmi Narayan Mittal

Lakshmi Narayan Mittal (Lakshmi Mittal), the Chairman and CEO of Arcelor Mittal was born on June 15, 1950 in Sadulpur village, in the Churu district of Rajasthan, India and is presently living in Kensington, London, United Kingdom for over 14 years. In 1969, with a Bachelors of Commerce degree in Business and Accounting, he graduated from St. Xavier's College in Kolkata, India; after which he joined his father's family steel business in the early 1970's. Later, he moved to Indonesia in 1976 and founded a Steel plant, Ispat Indo which proved to be very successful. In 1992, he acquired Mexico's third largest Steel producer, Sicartsa for $220 million and Siderurgicadel balsas SA at Lazaro Cardenas in Mexico and few other companies in Canada, Germany, Ireland, Trinidad and Tobago.

In 1997, he listed the company on the New York and Amsterdam Stock Exchange. He is married to Usha Mittal and has a son Aditya Mittal and a daughter Vanisha Mittal. His wife Usha runs the Indonesian business and his son Aditya and daughter Vanisha are members of the Board of Directors of Mittal Steel. He bought the Kensington Place Gardens in

London, for $128 million, which was the most expensive home in the world at that time. He is the richest person living in UK and Asia since 2005 and the fourth richest person on the earth with a total net worth of US $ 45 Billion. He is the President of the Board of Directors and Chief Executive Officer of Arcelor Mittal (the company is the world's largest producer of steel and is the combination of world's number one and number two steel company Arcelor and Mittal Steel). He is connected to 159 board members in 19 organizations across 5 different industries. His total annual compensation as of fiscal year 2007 is $4, 182, 000. In 2008 he was awarded Padma Vibhushan, the second most prestigious award in India; in 2007 he won Bessemer Gold Medal; whereas in 2006 Person of the Year by Financial Times and in 2004 European Businessman of the Year by Fortune magazine; previously in 1998 he received Willy Korf Steel Vision Award from American Metal Market and PaineWeber's World Steel Dynamics and in 1996 he was honoured as Steelmaker of the Year by New Steel. He believes, "Everyone experiences tough times, it is a measure of your determination and dedication how you deal with them and how you can come through them", he added, "Hard work certainly goes a long way. These days a lot of people work hard, so you have to make sure you work even harder and really dedicate yourself to what you are doing and setting out to achieve". On leadership and opportunities, he once said, "Always think outside the box and embrace opportunities that appear, wherever they might be. When people can see which direction the leaders are going in it becomes easier to motivate them."

8. Rahul Bajaj

Rahul Bajaj is an Executive Chairman and Head of Bajaj Group of companies of Bajaj Auto Ltd, Bajaj Group, which was started by Jamnalal Bajaj. The Bajaj Group diversified their businesses to automobiles, home appliances, lighting, iron and steel, insurance, travel and finance. Rahul Bajaj has one brother – Shishir Bajaj. He is married to Rupa Bajaj; and they have two sons – Rajiv and Sanjiv (who manages his company) and one daughter – Sunaina Kejriwal. He completed his schooling from Cathedral and John Connon School, Mumbai; St. Stephen's College, Delhi and Harvard University, U.S.A; and took control of Bajaj Group in 1965. Rahul Bajaj served as Managing Director of Bajaj Holdings and Investment Limited (formerly, Bajaj Auto Ltd) until 31 March, 2005. He is a Deputy General Manager of Bajaj Tempo Limited and Chairman of the Board of Bajaj Finserv Ltd., Bajaj Allianz Life Insurance Co., and Bajaj Allianz General Insurance Co. Ltd. He has been chairman of Bajaj Auto Finance Ltd since 26 July, 1972; and Non-executive Chairman of Bajaj Holdings & Investment Limited since February 20, 2008. He was the Executive Director of Bajaj Holdings and Investment Limited until February 2008.

He is a Member of International Advisory Committee of NYSE Euronext, Inc. (Formerly New York Stock Exchange, Inc.), and is a President of Confederation of Indian Industry.

He was also the President of Society of Indian Automobile Manufacturers (SIAM) and Mahratta Chamber of Commerce, Industry and Agriculture (MCCIA) and a Chairman of the Development Council for Automobiles and Allied Industries. He was elected to the Upper House of Parliament (Rajya Sabha) in June 2006 from Maharashtra. On 12th May, 2003 he was nominated by the President of India as the Chairman of the Board of Governors of the Indian Institute of Technology, Mumbai. He was the Chairman of the International Business Council of the World Economic Forum, Geneva. After the downfall in 2001, he started a factory in Chakan; invested in R&D and then introduced Bajaj Pulsar Motorcycle, which is currently one of the Leaders in its sector. Under his dynamic Leadership his company has risen from Rs. 72 million to Rs. 46.16 billion and he started manufacturing units at Akurdi and Waluj. He was listed 20th on the Forbes "India's richest 40" list of people with a net worth of US$ 1.1 Billion.

His awards are as follows:

- In 1975, he received the "Man of the Year" award from National Institute of Quality Assurance; he was awarded as "Businessman of the year 1985" by Business India; in 1988, he was recognised for his achievements by Pune Municipal Corporation and in 1990 he was rewarded by Bombay Management Association for his service in the field of Management.
- He was awarded India's one of the most prestigious award "Padma Bhushan" in 2001.
- His success mantra in life is, "Do whatever you think best, but be best at whatever you do".

9. Ratan Tata – A Visionary

"I am proud of my country. But we need to unite to make a unified India, free of communalism and casteism. We need to build India into a land of equal opportunity for all. We can be a truly great nation if we set our sights high and deliver to the people the fruits of continued growth, prosperity and equal opportunity" – Ratan Tata.

Ratan Naval Tata, presently Chairman of the **Tata Group** (India's one of the largest Company founded by Jamshedji Tata) was born on 28 December, 1937 in Mumbai, India.

Ratan Tata got his Bachelor's Science degree in Architecture from Cornell University. 1971, he was appointed as Director-in-Charge of NELCO (The National Radio and Electronics Company); in 1981 he was appointed as the Chairman of Tata Industries and in 1991 he took over as the Group Chairman from J.R.D. Tata. Under his dynamic leadership, the Tata group showed many notable/significant growths and development, some of which are:

1. Tata Consultancy Service went Public.
2. Tata Motors was listed on New York Stock Exchange.
3. Tata Indica was launched.

4. Tata acquired Corus group, an Anglo-Steel and Aluminum Producer.
5. Tata Nano (Rs. 1, 00,000) Car was launched.
6. Tata acquired Jaguar and Land Rover from Ford Motor Company.

Thus, with these achievements he converted his dreams into reality of making India an International name. He once said, "The country is now universally recognized as a nation on the move and takes its place amongst the successful economies in the region. The future potential is enormous but the country's destiny is in our hands. The time has come to move from small increments to bold, large initiatives. The time has come to stretch the envelope and set goals, which were earlier not seen to be possible. The time has come for performance to be measured and for allocated funds of the government to reach the people for whom they were intended".

His awards and recognition are as follow:

- On January 26, 2000 he was awarded Padma Bhushan.
- In 2007, Tata Family was rewarded with the Carnegie Media of Philanthropy (which was accepted by Ratan Tata).
- In November 2007, he was listed by Fortune magazine among the 25 Most Powerful People.
- On January 26, 2008 he was honored with Padma Vibhushan.
- On February 14, 2008 in Mumbai he received NASSCOM global Leadership Award.
- In 2008, he was among the 100 most Influential People in the Times Magazine.

Thus, an Entrepreneur, Industrialist, Leader, Role Model, Philanthropist and a Visionary not only for Tata group but also for India and the world. His Vision in life is "One hundred years from now, I expect the Tata's to be much bigger than it is now. More importantly, I hope the Group comes to be regarded as being the best in India. Best in the manner in which we operate, best in the products we deliver and best in our value systems and ethics. Having said that, I hope that a hundred years from now we will spread our wings far beyond India"

10. Narayan Murthy

"Performance leads to recognition. Recognition brings respect. Respect enhances power. Humility and grace in one's moments of power enhances dignity of an organization," – Narayan Murty N.R Narayan Murthy a bachelor of electrical engineering from university of Mysore and M.Tech from I.I.T Kanpur (born on 20 August, 1946 in Mysore, Karnataka, India.) He was the CEO of Infosys Technologies for 21 long years from 1981 to 2002. He is currently the non-executive chairman and chief mentor of Infosys. In February 2001, Infosys Technologies Ltd. (Infosys) was voted as the Best Managed Company in Asia in the Information Technology sector, in leading financial magazine Euro money's Fifth Annual Survey of Best Managed Companies in Asia.

Infosys started in 1981, by seven professional entrepreneurs led by Narayan Murthy, Chairman and CEO of Infosys with an equity capital of Rs.10, 000. By 2000, Infosys' market capitalization reached Rs.11 billion and by 2001, Infosys was one of the biggest exporters of software from India. Narayan Murthy built an organization that is respected across the country, with very strong systems, high ethical values and a nurtured work atmosphere. With his sound management skills, Murthy Infosys to the pinnacle of success in two decades. From a turnover of Rs.1.16 million in 1981, Infosys had grown to an Rs.19 billion company in 2001. There were many firsts to Narayan Murthy's credit. Infosys was the first company to push for off-shore software development (due to low hourly rates and technically well-trained programmers, the European and American organizations have their major software development projects done in less developed countries such as India) as against body shopping (It is contract labor of skilled workers. It refers to the practice of recruiting software professionals in India and sending them to work on projects abroad) that was coming during the 1980s. He championed corporate governance in India. Infosys was the first Indian company to follow the US Generally Accepted Accounting Principles (GAAP) disclosure norms before going for a NASDAQ listing in 1999. In 1987, Infosys entered into a joint venture with Kurt Salmon Associates (KSA), a leading global management consultancy firm. KSA-Infosys was the first Indo-American joint venture in the US. Analysts felt that one factor which helped Infosys to grow at a faster pace than others was the low employee turnover. The turnover rate at Infosys was around 11 per cent as opposed to industry average for software companies' of over 25 per cent during the 1990s. Infosys' retention capability was a function both of its rigorous selection procedures as well as proactive HRD practices. About 80 per cent of the middle and senior-level executives were promoted from within the organization. Narayan Murthy's vision for Infosys was, "I want Infosys to be a place where people of different genders, nationalities, races and religious beliefs work together in an environment of intense competition but utmost harmony, courtesy and dignity to add more and more value to our customers day after day." Infosys adopted the stringent US Generally Accepted Accounting Practices (GAAP) many years before other companies in India did. In August 2001, Narayan Murthy set up a Leadership Institute in Mysore, India, to manage the future growth of Infosys. The institute aimed at preparing Infosys employees to face the complexities of a rapidly changing marketplace and to bring about a change in work culture by instilling leadership qualities. He believed, "Our assets walk out of the door each evening. We have to make sure that they come back the next morning."

Follow Your Dream

Follow your dream.
Take one step at a time and don't settle for less,
Just continue to climb.
Follow your dream.
If you stumble, don't stop and lose sight of your goal
Press to the top.
For only on top can we see the whole view,
Can we see what we've done and what we can do;
Can we then have the vision to seek something new,
Press on.
Follow your dream.

—Amanda Bradley

Entrepreneurs Who made us Proud

Dr. **Karsanbhai Patel** manufactured a washing powder nirma in the backyard of his house. The cheapest detergent in the market was available for Rs. 13, he sold the product door to door at Rs 3 per kg to the middle and lower-income section of the society. Later in 1980's Nirma went ahead of Surf (a HUL brand) with more than 35% market share, in detergent market.

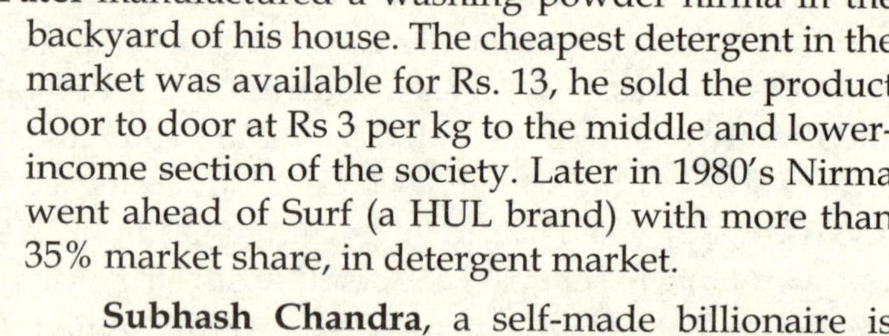

Subhash Chandra, a self-made billionaire is a role model for budding entrepreneurs. At the young age of 19, he started a vegetable oil unit; later expanded his business exporting food grains and entered into packaging business. In 1988; he set up Essel World; followed by Water Kingdom in 1988; and Zee TV in 1992. He was the pioneer in starting ICL (Indian Cricket Legue).

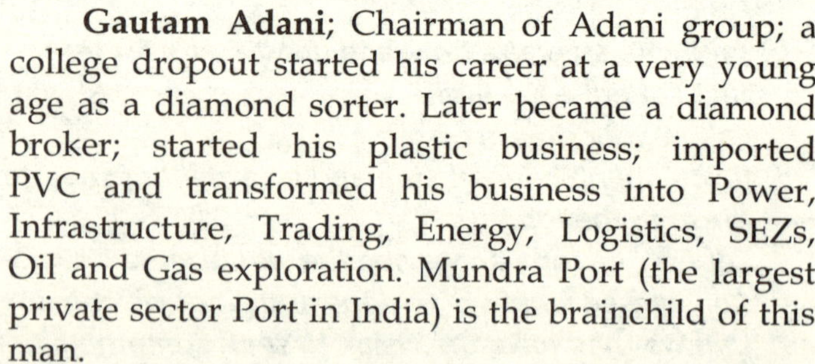

Gautam Adani; Chairman of Adani group; a college dropout started his career at a very young age as a diamond sorter. Later became a diamond broker; started his plastic business; imported PVC and transformed his business into Power, Infrastructure, Trading, Energy, Logistics, SEZs, Oil and Gas exploration. Mundra Port (the largest private sector Port in India) is the brainchild of this man.

Other inspiring business tycoons in India are as follows: Reading about their lives can be a great source of motivation for many.

1. **Adi Godrej**, Chairman of Godrej group.
2. **Sammer Gehlaut**, Founder of India Bulls.
3. **KP Singh**, Founder of DLF.
4. **Ramesh Chandra**, the Real Estate Mogul and founder of Unitech.

5. **Kumar Mangalam Birla**, Chairman of Aditya Birla Group.
6. **Tulsi Tanti**, Chairman and Managing Director of Suzlon.
7. **Kiran Mazumdar Shaw**, Chairman and Managing Director of Biocon.
8. **Pallonji Mistry**, Chairman of Shapoorji Pallonji Group.
9. **Lalit Suri**, Chairman of the Bharat Hotels.
10. **Bhai Mohan Singh**, Founder of Ranbaxy Laboratories Ltd.

Here, are 11 International influential business magnates that broke all rules of business and created History in their own way:

1. **Jack Welch** named "Manager of the Century" for reorganizing GE.
2. **Sam Watson** founder of Wal Mart.
3. **Donald Trump**, Chairman and CEO of Trump Organization.
4. **Ray Kroc**, founder of Mc Donald Restaurant.
5. **Arkadi Kuhlmann**, founder and CEO of ING Direct in USA.
6. **Sergey Brin** and **Larry Page**, founder of Google Search Engine.
7. **Steve Jobs**, Co- founder of APPLE and Chairman of Pixar.
8. **Bill Gates**, Co-founder of Microsoft.
9. **Henry Ford**, founder of Ford Motor Company.
10. **Andrew Carnegie**, founder of Carnegie Steel Company.
11. **Michael Dell**, founder and CEO of Dell Inc.

Start Where You Stand

Start where you stand and never mind the past,
The past won't help you in beginning new,
If you have left it all behind at last
Why, that's enough, you're done with it, you're through;
This is another chapter in the book;
This is another race that you have planned,
Don't give the vanished days a backward look,
Start where you stand.
The world won't care about your old defeats
If you can start anew and win success;
The future is your time, and time is fleet
And there is much of work and strain and stress;
Forget the buried woes and dead despairs,
Here is a brand-new trial right at hand,
The future is for him who does and dares,
Start where you stand.

—Berton Braley

11 Stories that Inspire and Motivate us to Achieve our Goals!!!

STORY 1

There was a rich merchant who had 4 wives. He loved his forth wife the most and adorned her with rich clothes and treated her to delicacies. He took great care of her and gave her nothing but the best.

He also loved his third wife very much. He was very proud of her and always wanted to show off her to his friends. However, the merchant was always in great fear that she might run away with somebody.

He too, loved his second wife. She is a very considerate person, always patient and in fact was the merchant's confidante. Whenever the merchant faced any problems, he always turned to his second wife and she would always help him out and tide him through difficult times.

Now, the merchant's first wife was a very loyal partner and has made great contributions in maintaining his wealth and business as well as took care of the household. However, the merchant did not love the first wife although she loved him deeply.

One day, the merchant fell ill. Before long, he knew that he was going to die soon. He thought of his luxurious life and told himself, "Now I have four wives with me. But when I die, I'll be alone. How lonely I'll be!"

Thus, he asked his fourth wife, "I loved you the most, endowed you with the finest clothing and showered great care over you. Now that I'm dying, will you follow me and keep me company?" "No way!" replied the fourth wife and she walked away without another word.

The answer cut like a sharp knife right into the merchant's heart. The sad merchant then asked the third wife, "I have loved you so much all my life. Now that I'm dying, will you follow me and keep me company?" "No!" replied the third wife. "Life is so good over here! I'm going to remarry when you die!" The merchant's heart sank and turned cold.

He then asked the second wife, "I always turned to you for help and you've always helped me out. Now I need your help again. When I die, will you follow me and keep me company?" "I'm sorry, I can't help you out this time!" replied the second wife. "At the very most, I can only send you to your grave." The answer came like a bolt of thunder and the merchant was devastated.

Then a voice called out: "I'll leave with you. I'll follow you no matter where you go." The merchant looked up and there was his first wife. She was so skinny, almost like she suffered from malnutrition. Greatly grieved, the merchant said, "I should have taken much better care of you while I could have!"

Actually, we all have four partners in our lives:

a. The forth partner is our body. No matter how much time and effort we lavish in making it look good, it'll leave us when we die.

b. Our third partner? Our possessions, status and wealth. When we die, they all go to others.

c. The second partner is our family and friends. No matter how close they had been there for us when we're alive, the furthest they can stay by us is up to the grave.

d. The first partner is in fact our soul, often neglected in our pursuit of material, wealth and sensual pleasure.

It is actually the only thing that follows us wherever we go. Perhaps it's a good idea to cultivate and strengthen it now rather than to wait until we're on our deathbed to lament.

STORY 2

In 1883, a creative engineer named John Roebling was inspired by the idea of building a spectacular bridge connecting New York with Long Island. However bridge building experts throughout the world thought that this was an impossible feat and told Roebling to forget the idea. It just could not be done. It was not practical. It had never been done before.

Roebling could not ignore the vision he had in his mind of this bridge. He thought about it all the time and he knew deep in his heart that it could be done. He just had to share the dream with someone who had faith in him.

After much discussion and persuasion he managed to convince his son Washington, engineer, that the bridge in fact could be built. Working together for the first time, the father and son developed concepts of how it could be accomplished and how the obstacles could be overcome. With great excitement and inspiration, and the headiness of a wild challenge before them, they hired their crew and began to build their dream bridge.

The project started well, but when it was only a few months underway a tragic accident on the site killed John Roebling. Washington was injured and left with a certain amount of brain damage, which resulted in him not being able to walk or talk.

"We told them so."

"Crazy men and their crazy dreams."

"It's foolish to chase wild visions."

Everyone had a negative comment to make and felt that the project should be scrapped since the Roebling's were the only ones who knew how the bridge could be built. In spite of his handicap Washington was never discouraged and still had a burning desire to complete the bridge and his mind was still as sharp as ever.

He tried to inspire and pass on his enthusiasm to some of his friends, but they were too daunted by the task. As he lay on his bed in his hospital room, with the sunlight streaming through the windows, a gentle breeze blew the flimsy white curtains apart and he was able to see the sky and the tops of the trees outside for just a moment.

It seemed that there was a message for him not to give up. Suddenly an idea hit him. All he could do was move one finger and he decided to make the best use of it. By moving this, he slowly developed a code of communication with his wife.

He touched his wife's arm with that finger, indicating to her that he wanted her to call the engineers again. Then he used the same method of tapping her arm to tell the engineers what to do. It seemed foolish but the project was under way again.

For thirteen years, Washington tapped out his instructions with his finger on his wife's arm, until the bridge was finally completed. Today the spectacular Brooklyn Bridge stands in all its glory as a tribute to the triumph of one man's indomitable spirit and his determination not to be defeated by circumstances. It is also a tribute to the engineers and their team work, and to their faith in a man who was considered mad by half the world. It stands too as a tangible monument to the love and devotion of his wife who for thirteen long years patiently decoded the messages of her husband and told the engineers what to do.

Perhaps this is one of the best examples of a never-say-die attitude that overcame physical handicap to achieve an impossible goal.

Often when we face obstacles in our day-to-day life, our hurdles seem very small in comparison to what many others have to face. The Brooklyn

Bridge shows us dreams that seemed impossible could be realized with determination and persistence, no matter what the odds were. Even the most distant dream can be realized with determination and persistence.

STORY 3

Two men, both seriously ill, occupied the same hospital room. One man was allowed to sit up in his bed for an hour a day to drain the fluids from his lungs. His bed was next to the room's only window. The other man had to spend all his time flat on his back.

The men talked for hours on end. They spoke of their wives and families, their homes, their jobs, their involvement in the military service, where they had been on vacation. And every afternoon when the man in the bed next to the window could sit up, he would pass the time by describing to his roommate all the things he could see outside the window.

The man in the other bed would live for those one-hour periods where his world would be broadened and enlivened by all the activity and colour of the outside world. The window overlooked a park with a lovely lake, the man had said. Ducks and swans played on the water while children sailed their model boats. Lovers walked arm in arm amid flowers of every colour of the rainbow.

Grand old trees graced the landscape, and a fine view of the city skyline could be seen at a distance. As the man by the window described all this in exquisite detail, the man on the other side of the room would close his eyes and imagine the picturesque scene.

One warm afternoon the man by the window described a parade passing by. Although the other man could not hear the band, he could see it in his mind's eye as the gentleman by the window portrayed it with descriptive words. Unexpectedly, an alien thought entered his head: Why should he have all the pleasure of seeing everything while I never get to see anything? It didn't seem fair.

As the thought fermented, the man felt ashamed at first. But as the days passed and he missed seeing more sights, his envy eroded into resentment and soon turned him sour. He began to brood and found himself unable to sleep. He should be by that window — and that thought now controlled his life.

Late one night, as he lay staring at the ceiling, the man by the window began to cough. He was choking on the fluid in his lungs. The other man watched in the dimly lit room as the struggling man by the window groped for the button to call for help.

Listening from across the room, he never moved, never pushed his own button which would have brought the nurse running. In less than five minutes, the coughing and choking stopped, along with the sound of breathing. Now, there was only silence—deathly silence.

The following morning, the day nurse arrived to bring water for their baths. When she found the lifeless body of the man by the window, she was saddened and called the hospital attendant to take it away—no words, no fuss. As soon as it seemed appropriate, the man asked if he could be moved next to the window. The nurse was happy to make the switch and after making sure he was comfortable, she left him alone.

Slowly, painfully, he propped himself up on one elbow to take his first look. Finally, he could enjoy the sight it all by himself. He strained to slowly look out of the window. It faced a blank wall.

The pursuit of happiness is a matter of choice...it is a positive attitude we consciously choose to express. It is not a gift that gets delivered to our doorstep each morning, nor does it come through the window. And I am certain that our circumstances are just a small part of what makes us joyful. If we wait for them to get just right, we will never find lasting joy.

The pursuit of happiness is an inward journey. If we regularly deposit positive, encouraging, and uplifting thoughts, if we continue to bite our lips just before we begin to grumble and complain, if we shoot down that seemingly harmless negative thought as it germinates, we will find that there is much to rejoice about.

STORY 4

A man found a cocoon of a butterfly. One day a small opening appeared. He sat and watched the butterfly for several hours as it struggled to force its body through that little hole. Then it seemed to stop making any progress. It appeared as if it had gotten as far as it could, and it could go no further.

So the man decided to help the butterfly. He took a pair of scissors and snipped off the remaining bit of the cocoon. The butterfly then emerged easily. But it had a swollen body and small, shriveled wings.

The man continued to watch the butterfly because he expected that, at any moment, the wings would enlarge and expand to be able to support the body, which would contract in time.

Neither happened! In fact, the butterfly spent the rest of its life crawling around with a swollen body and shriveled wings. It never was able to fly.

What the man, in his kindness and haste, did not understand was that the restricting cocoon and the struggle required for the butterfly to get through the tiny opening were God's way of forcing fluid from the body of the butterfly into its wings so that it would be ready for flight once it achieved its freedom from the cocoon.

Sometimes struggles are exactly what we need in our lives. If God allowed us to go through our lives without any obstacles, it would cripple us. We would not be as strong as what we could have been. We could never fly!

STORY 5

In ancient times, a king had a boulder placed on a roadway. Then he hid himself and watched to see if anyone would remove the huge rock. Some of the king's wealthiest merchants and courtiers came by and simply walked around it.

Many loudly blamed the king for not keeping the roads clear, but none did anything about getting the big stone out of the way. Then a peasant came along carrying a load of vegetables. On approaching the boulder, the peasant laid down his burden and tried to move the stone to the side of the road. After much pushing and straining, he finally succeeded. As the peasant picked up his load of vegetables, he noticed a purse lying in the road where the boulder had been. The purse contained many gold coins and a note from the king indicating that the gold was for the person who removed the boulder from the roadway.

The peasant learned what other failed.

Every obstacle presents an opportunity to improve one's condition.

STORY 6

A well-known speaker started off his seminar by holding up a $20 bill. In the room of 200, he asked, "Who would like this $20 bill?" Hands started going up.

He said, "I am going to give this $20 to one of you but first, let me do this." He proceeded to crumple the dollar bill up. He then asked, "Who still wants it?" Still the hands were up in the air.

"Well," he replied, "What if I do this?" And he dropped it on the ground and started to grind it into the floor with his shoe. He picked it up, now all crumpled and dirty. "Now who still wants it?" Still the hands went into the air.

"My friends, you have all learned a very valuable lesson. No matter what I did to the money, you still wanted it because it did not decrease in value. It was still worth $20.

Many times in our lives, we are dropped, crumpled, and dirty by the decisions we make and the circumstances that come our way.

We feel as though we are worthless. But no matter what has happened or what will happen, you will never lose your value. You are special – Don't ever forget it!

STORY 7

A professor once stood before his class with some items on the table. When the class began, wordlessly he picked up a large and empty mayonnaise jar and proceeded to fill it with rocks, about 2 inches in diameter.

He then asked the students if the jar was full. They agreed that it was.

So the professor then picked up a box of pebbles and poured them into the jar. He shook the jar lightly. The pebbles, of course, rolled into the open areas between the rocks. He then asked the students again if the jar was full. They agreed it was.

The professor picked up a box of sand and poured it into the jar. Of course, the sand filled up everything else. He then asked once more if the jar was full. The students responded with a unanimous "Yes."

"Now," said the professor, "I want you to recognize that this jar represents your life. The rocks are the important things – your family, your partner, your health, your children – things that if everything else was lost and only they remained, your life would still be full.

The pebbles are the other things that matter – like your job, your house, your car.

The sand is everything else. The small stuff."

"If you put the sand into the jar first," he continued "there is no room for the pebbles or the rocks. The same goes for your life.

If you spend your time and energy on small stuffs, you will never have room for the things that are important to you. Pay attention to the things that are critical to your happiness. Play with your children. Take your partner out dancing. There will always be time to go to work, clean the house, give a dinner party and fix the disposal.

Take care of the rocks first – the things that really matter. Set your priorities. The rest is only sand."

STORY 8

Chuan and Jing joined a wholesale company together just after graduation. Both worked very hard.

After several years, the boss promoted Jing to the position of sales executive but Chuan remained a sales rep. One day, Chuan could not take it anymore, tendered resignation to the boss and complained the boss did not value hard working staff, but only promoted those who flattered him.

The boss knew that Chuan worked very hard for the years, but in order to help Chuan realize the difference between him and Jing, the boss asked Chuan to do the following. Go and find out anyone selling water melon in the market? Chuan returned and said yes. The boss asked how much per kg? Chuan went back to the market to ask and returned to inform boss that it is $12 per kg.

Boss told Chuan, I will ask Jing the same question? Jing went, returned and said, boss, only one person is selling water melon. $12 per kg, $100 for 10 kg, he has inventory of 340 melons. On the table there are 58 melons, every melon weighs about 15 kg, are bought from the south two days ago, and are fresh and red, good quality.

Chuan was very impressed and realized the difference between himself and Jing. He decided not to resign but to learn from Jing.

A more successful person is more observant, thinks more and understands in depth. For the same matter, a successful person sees several years ahead, while others see only tomorrow. The difference between a year and a day is 365 times, how could you win?

STORY 9

Thomas Edison tried two thousand different materials in search of a filament for the light bulb. When none worked satisfactorily, his assistant complained, "All our work is in vain. We have learned nothing."

Edison replied confidently, "Oh, we have come a long way and we have learned a lot. We know that there are two thousand elements which we cannot use to make a good light bulb."

STORY 10

Mahatma Gandhi went from city to city, village to village collecting funds for Charkha Sangh. During one of his tours, he addressed a meeting in Orissa. After his speech was over a poor old woman who was bent with age, her hair was grey and clothes were in tatters got up.

The volunteers tried to stop her, but she fought her way to where Gandhiji was sitting. "I must see him," she insisted and going up to Gandhiji touched his feet. Then from the folds of her sari she brought out a copper coin and placed it at his feet. Gandhiji picked up the copper coin and put it away carefully.

The Charkha Sangh funds were under the charge of Jamnalal Bajaj. He asked Gandhiji for the coin but Gandhiji refused. "I keep cheques worth thousands of rupees for the Charkha Sangh," Jamnalal Bajaj said laughingly, "yet you won't trust me with a copper coin."

"This copper coin is worth much more than those thousands," Gandhiji said. "If a man has several lakhs and he gives away a thousand or two, it doesn't mean much. But this coin was perhaps all that the poor woman possessed. She gave me all she had. That was very generous of her. What a great sacrifice she made. That is why I value this copper coin more than thousands of rupees."

STORY 11

A young man was about to graduate. For many months he had admired a beautiful sports car in a dealer's showroom, and knowing his father could well afford it, he told him that was all he wanted. As Graduation Day approached, the young man awaited signs that his father had purchased the car. Finally, on the morning of his graduation his father called him into his private study. His father told him how proud he was to have such a fine son, and told him how much he loved him. He handed his son a beautiful wrapped gift box.

Curious, but somewhat disappointed the young man opened the box and found a lovely, leather-bound Bible. Angrily, he raised his voice at his father and said, "With all your money you give me a Bible?" and stormed out of the house, leaving the holy book. Many years passed and the young man was very successful in business. He had a beautiful home and wonderful family, but realized his father was very old, and thought perhaps he should go to him. He had not seen him since that graduation day. Before he could make arrangements, he received a telegram telling him his father had passed away, and willed all of his possessions to his son.

He needed to come home immediately and take care of his things. When he arrived at his father's house, sudden sadness and regret filled his heart.

He began to search his father's important papers and saw the still new Bible, just as he had left it years ago. With tears, he opened the Bible and began to turn the pages. As he read those words, a car key dropped from an envelope taped behind the Bible. It had a tag with the dealer's name, the same dealer who had the sports car he had desired. On the tag was the date of his graduation, and the words...PAID IN FULL.

How many times do we miss God's blessings because they are not packaged as we expected? Think about it.......

Before You

Before you speak, listen.
Before you write, think.
Before you spend, earn.
Before you invest, investigate.
Before you criticize, wait.
Before you pray, forgive.
Before you quit, try.
Before you retire, save.
Before you die, give.

—William Arthur Ward

Lets Get Inspired

Imagine life as a game in which you are juggling 5 balls in the air. You name them - work, family, health, friends and spirit and you're keeping all of these in the air. You will soon understand that work is a rubber ball. If you drop it, it will bounce back. But the other four balls – family, health, friends and spirit are made of glass. If you drop one of these, they will be irrevocably scuffed, marked, nicked, damaged or even shattered. They will never be the same. You must understand that and strive for balance in your life. How?

Coca Cola CEO Braian Dyson shared some inspiring words that will motivate, inspire and face life as it is:

- Don't undermine your worth by comparing yourself with others. It is because we are different that each of us is special.
- Don't set your goals by what other people deem important. Only you know what is best for you.
- Don't take for granted the things closest to your heart. Cling to them as you would your life, for without them, life is meaningless.
- Don't let your life slip through your fingers by living in the past or for the future. By living your life one day at a time, you live ALL the days of your life.
- Don't give up when you still have something to give. Nothing is really over until the moment you stop trying.
- Don't be afraid to admit that you are less than perfect. It is this fragile thread that binds us each together.

- Don't be afraid to encounter risks. It is by taking chances that we learn how to be brave.
- Don't shut love out of your life by saying it's impossible to find. The quickest way to receive love is to give; the fastest way to lose love is to hold it too tightly; and the best way to keep love is to give it wings.
- Don't run through life so fast that you forget not only where you've been, but also where you are going.
- Don't forget that a person's greatest emotional need is to feel appreciated.
- Don't be afraid to learn. Knowledge is weightless, a treasure you can always carry easily.
- Don't use time or words carelessly. Neither can be retrieved. Life is not a race, but a journey to be savoured each step of the way.

8 Articles on Motivation By Prominent Speakers

The author must mention the source of the articles. These articles are clean since they've been taken from original international articles. I recently read few immensely motivating and inspiring articles which I would like to share with you:

1. Pacing Your Day and Life

Life is a marathon, and not a sprint; however, there are times – even in a marathon – when sprinting is required. Most of us in the 21st century have very complex professional and personal lives. Our ancestors often went to work and did one thing at a set pace all day. Then they went home to their families only to go back to work and do the same thing the following day.

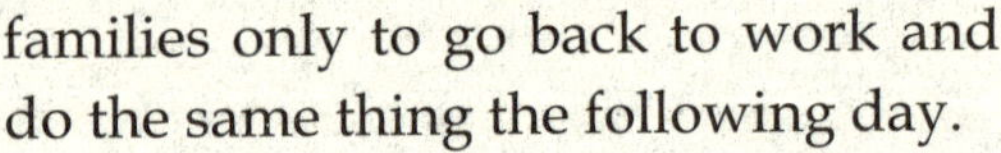

Today, most of us juggle a myriad of professional projects and personal responsibilities. The time and boundaries between work and family or personal and professional have blurred. We have become very project-oriented. This causes us to deal with concepts, schedules, and deadlines. These must be managed delicately for us to succeed.

If you will remember being in college or even high school, you had a number of subjects taught by a number of teachers, each requiring you to prepare projects, papers, and study for tests. Going through that educational process, it seemed to me that there were times it ran very smoothly – almost as if all the teachers or professors had gotten together behind the scenes to coordinate my semester or school year.

On the other hand, it seemed like there were other times when I faced the same course load, but I felt as if all the teachers or professors had gotten together in a secret meeting to conspire against me. It seemed as if they organized tests as well as due dates for papers and projects to conflict with one another.

Of course, I realize now, looking back, that none of my teachers or professors gave any thought to me one way or the other when they scheduled their courses. Just as the people who control deadlines, workflow, and budgets for our work lives or those who schedule kids' sports practices and other church, family, and social events, don't secretly conspire against us.

At best, our work and home lives are challenging and hectic to manage, but there are a few ideas that may help us:

- Prioritize the most important things and be prepared to eliminate the lowest priorities if everything becomes too chaotic.
- Pull things forward in your calendar and get them out of the way during slack times in other projects. In this way, you can begin to control deadlines, even though they are set by other people.
- Make others around you aware of all the commitments you already have so they can consider your schedule in light of overall responsibilities.
- Realize that there are going to be times when you are required to sprint, but you can't do that throughout an entire marathon or your whole life.
- Your schedule ultimately belongs to you and is your responsibility. You have more control than you think you have.
- As you go through your day today, sprint when it is required but only as a part of the overall plan to win your personal and professional marathon.

Today is the day!

—Jim Stovall

2. The Power of Patience

Are you like me and you want your dream to be manifested now? Do you find yourself creating drama, struggle and doubt when your goals aren't realized fast enough?

The universal truth about achievement is "Success is a process."

Get that in your thick skull and receive it in your heart. The sooner you accept this truth, the more powerful you will be in your service to others, the more fun you will have, and ironically, the 'quicker' you'll attract results.

Several weeks ago I taught this principle to my coaching clients on a group call and the results have been extraordinary! When you can let go and surrender to the process; when you release your attachment to your goals, you create an ability to see things you would have missed.

Take this principle to heart today and you open a portal for the supernatural to guide, direct and empower you and the reality of your dreams.

Creating success is a process

The Law of Gestations says, "Ideas, goals and desires are spiritual seeds and they always move into form or a physical result."

In other words, "Your goals will manifest. Your dreams will happen." The problem with this Universal Truth is most of us plant seeds (ideas, goals and dreams) and, if we don't see a plant within a short period of time, we dig up the seed to see what's wrong! Or, we leave that seed and go plant another one!

But you never do that... right?

When you can accept that success is a process, your goals will manifest in due time, you will be able to stay focused, remain committed and continue to act in creating them.

Consider this:

A human baby takes about 42 weeks to grow full-term.

A carrot seed takes about 72 days.

Chicken eggs take about 21 days to hatch.

A caterpillar takes 10 days to 3 weeks to turn into a butterfly.

Knowing that the process is happening, even if you can't 'see' the result is an important aspect to creating success.

Create a powerful stand for the seeds you've planted and choose to "fall in love" with the process of creation!

Here's the process I taught my coaching clients that gave them such great results:

4 Steps to creating what you desire

Step 1: Decide what you want and write it down and make a vision board. Decision means "to cut off". Be bold. Be brave. Make a decision. Focus intention. Plant the seed you really want and know with certainty that the seed will harvest when you cultivate it. It's the Law!

Step 2: Feel the emotion. Act as if you already possess the things pictured on your vision board – the house, the car, the dream partner, results in your business. Say, "This" is already mine. State your goals in the present tense like you have already achieved them. "I am so happy and grateful for..." "I am the owner of an Ocean front Home!" "The leader of a profitable Organization with 100,000 people or more!" "I am the #1 Salesman in my company."

Step 3: Choose your "Way of Being" Leadership! You are the leader you're waiting for! Look at your vision board and ask yourself, "Who does this person living this life need to be?" Ways of being: I am grateful, leader, inspiration, joy, generous, focus, contribution, energy! Create your 'way of being' every day: Mine is, "I am global leadership and I make a difference!"

Step 4: Obey inspired action! You will receive a "call to action" this week. My coaching for you is to "obey it!" Take action. When you 'obey' the inspired action, the next step will be revealed to you.

> ***"The universe likes speed. Don't delay. Don't second guess. Don't doubt. When the opportunity is there, when the impulse is there, when the intuitive nudge from within is there, act. That's your job. And that's all you have to do."***
>
> *—Dr. Joe Vitale*

Create a powerful stand for the seeds you've planted and choose to "Fall in Love" with the process of Creation!

Choose to release struggle, frustration and doubt and take on your new way of being... Faith! Power! Intention! ... knowing that the seeds you have planted (your goals and desires) will come to fruition.

Make it a miraculous day!

—Lisa Jimenez

3. Five Strategies to Help Escape "The Box"

It is often said that people are afraid of change, but that's not true. People love change – as it comes with a guarantee that it's going to be a positive change.

To prove this to yourself, imagine a change that entails a zero being added to the dollar figure on your paycheck, no strings attached. Most people dream of such changes! This is, of course, a hypothetical example.

People are not afraid of change per se - what they are afraid of is the uncertainty that goes with change. That is why so many people never venture very far from their own little box.

Here are five strategies that will help you get out of whatever box you happen to be making your own mental home right now:

1. **Embrace uncertainty:** My values coach colleague Dick Schwab says that people must choose either the certainty of misery or the misery of uncertainty. Dr. Edward Hallowell, author of the book *Worry,* describes the anxiety-performance curve which demonstrates that - up to a point – anxiety can inspire positive performance but after that point, the impact can be seriously negative (recall your worst case of test anxiety).

   You cannot make anxiety and fear go away (according to the late Dr. M. Scott Peck, the absence of fear is not courage, its brain damage). What you can do is make fear your ally by letting it prod you to take action toward your most important goals.

2. **Create prototypes:** There's nothing you can do that can't be done – if you think big and start small (with apologies to the Beatles). The best way to do that is by using prototype thinking to create models (mental and physical) that move you along the path.

   If your goal is to write a book, a prototype could be a magazine article, or even a letter to the editor (anything that will earn you that first rejection letter so you can start getting that fear under control).

3. **Look for fingerprints:** Tony Robbins says that success leaves fingerprints, but sometimes they're not left by the usual suspects. The founder of amazon.com founder Jeff Bezos did not invent the Internet (Al Gore did that), but he did find fingerprints of success in what other Internet companies were doing and applied it in a very new way.

4. **Avoid the dream stealers:** We have been told that if you have a bucket full of crabs and one of them tries to crawl out, the others will grab it and pull it back down. If you want to get out of the box, you might need to change your reference group (that's the sociologist's term for the people you hang around with).

5. **Dare most when times are darkest:** When Lee Iacocca became CEO of the failing Chrysler car company, he didn't do what most CEOs would have done in that situation - slash jobs. Instead, he launched one of the most audacious new car development projects in the history of the industry, giving us the K-car and the minivan — and saving the company in the process.

—Joe Tye

4. The Importance of Being Tenacious!

"Nothing in this world can take the place of persistence. Talent will not; nothing is more common than unsuccessful people with talent. Genius will not; unrewarded genius is almost a proverb. Education will not; the world is full of educated derelicts. Persistence and determination alone are omnipotent. The slogan 'press on' has solved and always will solve the problems of the human race."

—Calvin Coolidge

I have worked with many successful people; people who have achieved the kinds of lives they have dreamed about. I have also worked with many people who are not anywhere near where they want to be in life. Many times those who are not successful resent those who are and believe that somehow success was handed to those who have achieved much.

What I have found however is that actually the reverse is true. Those who have achieved much have worked much HARDER than those who are not successful. You wouldn't believe the stories of struggle that I hear from those who now appear to on "top of the heap."

Yes, they are successful, but no, it wasn't handed to them! And I find that most unsuccessful people who come to me actually haven't been tenacious at all. I find that with many of the people I speak to who complain about their lack of success simply haven't persevered and been tenacious.

When I ask them questions I usually get excuses. Yes, there are exceptions on both sides, but I find this to be almost universally true.

If you are one who finds yourself dreaming of a better life, or looking at someone who "has it made," I would ask you to take a long, deep look inward and at your life to find whether or not you have actually been tenacious in pursuit of your dreams.

How long have you gone for it? Many people who achieve much go for YEARS before they achieve what their hearts long for? How hard have you gone for it? Most people who achieve much have given up much. They have sacrificed much. They strive valiantly for what it is that resides deep in their dreams. They just plain ol' work hard!

So what are the principles of tenacity? What do you need to know in order to take your turn at the tenacious? Here are some thoughts to start your fire and get you going!

Sometimes you just have to outlast the others.

"Success seems to be largely a matter of hanging on after others have let go."

—William Feather

I have found that many people start on their dreams but most never finish. Then those who stop resent those who make it. The truth is that most people who become successful have simply mastered the art of keeping on keeping on! I myself can remember early on in my career when I would get discouraged and I literally said to myself, "One more week. Just give it one more week." Quite frankly, this is what got me through a couple of years of my work early on. I hung on as others let go.

It is easy to get disheartened. Ask those who have achieved success if they ever got disheartened and you will find some of the most amazing stories you have ever heard. Give it a try: Go to the most successful person you know and ask them if they ever thought about quitting. Ask them how they kept on going. You will be amazed at what you hear. Sometimes you just have to hold on at the end.

"When you get to the end of your rope, tie a knot and hang on."

—Franklin Roosevelt

I wonder how many people have quit just as they would have begun their entrance into success? Sure there are many who quit at the first sign of hard work, but what about those who, after the tenth time of trial then give up, just as fate would have seen them go through one last hurdle and then into the promised land?

How many people were on their last hurdle and decided not to jump? How many people had just one more mountain pass to go? Or just one more river to cross?

Of course we will never know, but certainly some of the people who quit are doing so on what would have been their last trial, right?

So what does this mean for you? For me it means I do not quit because I would hate to find out later that all I needed was just one last effort and I would have achieved my goal. What if it isn't my last trial? That's okay because as long as I keep going, eventually I will get to my last trial, I will overcome it, and I will enter the Winner's Circle.

Sometimes the most beautiful results come from dull things under pressure.

"Diamonds are nothing more than chunks of coal that stuck to their jobs."

—Malcolm Forbes

If coal wasn't an inanimate object it would certainly scream, "Stop! I want out!" But that coal, when facing incredible pressure, is turned into one of earth's most precious possessions. Ugly, dirty old coal is transformed into beautiful diamonds.

Instead of looking at pressure and trials as the reason to quit, get tenacious and see them as the very thing that will make your life the beautiful thing that you desire it to be. See it as your opportunity to learn, to grow, and to be transformed. See these trials as the very things that will enable you to have the life you dream of!

Trials will surely come. Life will get hard. You will want to quit.

Then you will have a choice: Will you give up? Or will you take your turn at tenacious. The choice you make will determine much of the rest of your life.

My advice? Take your turn at tenacious. You will become stronger, and you will end up living the life you dream of!

—Chris Widener

5. A Dead End is a Good Place to Turn Around

When I was a child my father loved to take us for rides on Sunday afternoons. Rarely did we have any idea where we were going or might end up. As we wandered along the roads, back roads and even cow tracks near our town, we often found ourselves in strange places.

More than once we ended up on a road that ended in the middle of nowhere or that came to an abrupt end at a barbed wire fence. When that happened, my dad simply laughed, turned the car around and said, "Well, at least we know where we aren't going."

Life is often like our aimless Sunday afternoon drives—the roads we travel may take us to some unknown or unanticipated places, and we can find ourselves on a dead end road. At that point we have the same choice my dad did—we can either stay stuck where we are, or we can take it in good humor and turn around.

Which direction to go is often our biggest dilemma. The choices we make are often determined by what we think we can do or achieve, and what we will allow ourselves to have. This, in turn, is often determined by what we think of ourselves, much of which has been instilled in us and programmed by others.

Ben W. is a perfect example. Nothing ever seemed to quite work out for him. As an adult, he struggled with relationships, and after three failed marriages, gave up on the whole idea. He could never keep a job either, or hold onto money. To Ben, life was totally unfair—other people always got the breaks, and everyone just had it in for him.

As a child he had been bullied at school by his classmates and repeatedly punished by teachers who told him he was lazy and stupid. At home he was labeled a "screw up" and a dummy, and was constantly reminded by his family that he was "no good" and would never amount to anything. At 16 Ben had an argument with his third stepmother, which resulted in his father throwing him out and telling him to get out of their lives and not come back.

As a result, Ben dropped out of school, lived on the streets for a time, and to ease his anxiety and despair, got involved with drugs and alcohol. The only emotion Ben felt comfortable expressing was anger, and there were plenty of opportunities for him to do that. He was truly heading for a dead end.

Then, through a series of unforeseen circumstances, Ben came to the attention of a kindly man who began to help Ben turn his life around. Encouraged by his new mentor, Ben gradually began to make changes in his life. These were small steps at first, followed by bigger ones as time went on. For the first time ever he had someone to believe in him. As he began to experience the transforming power of unconditional love and acceptance, he eventually started believing in himself.

It was a life-altering experience.

Like Ben, we may have to experience our own catastrophe to make us realize we too need to turn around. It can often take a metaphorical two by four to the head to make us pay attention and realize that if we truly want life to get better, we cannot stay stuck where we are. It comes down to a conscious choice.

We can either do what we've always done—keep making the same old mistakes, wallowing in self pity, hanging out with the complainers and lamenting our misfortunes in life, or we can start pulling ourselves up.

How and where do you start?

1. Examine your thoughts and beliefs. What kind of negative self talk goes on in your head and what is your opinion of yourself? Do you constantly put yourself down and beat yourself up for your shortcomings? What was your family's opinion of you and what did you hear over and over when you were a child? If you learned early in life to think of yourself as a loser, are undeserving or worthless, your life undoubtedly reflects that.

2. Stop thinking of yourself as a victim and quit blaming others for your circumstances. Start taking responsibility for your own actions; acknowledge you have played a major role in getting where you are. It no longer matters what you did in the past—the only thing that matters now is what you are going to do about the future.

3. Who might be able to help you? Do you have a role model or someone you admire—at home, church, school or work who might be willing to lend a hand, brainstorm ideas with you, or become a mentor? Recognizing when you need help and being willing to ask for it is a sign of strength, not weakness.

4. Stop making excuses and start making a plan. Even if you think you have no options, you need to change your mind about

that too. It is easy to fall back on old excuses. It's the economy. It's my family. There are no other jobs. I'm not good enough. I don't have any money. It is not possible. This is just how it is.

The real truth is, no matter what our circumstances are, we still have choices no matter how small they seem. In a single day, we make hundreds of choices about hundreds of things, even if they seem so insignificant they are unnoticeable. We can choose to stay in bed or ignore the alarm clock. We can wear this outfit or that one. We can clean the kitchen or watch TV. We can call a friend, or wallow in misery all by ourselves. And so it goes. Your job is to come up with a list of things you can do that will start turning you around and heading in a different direction. You may be surprised at how many there are.

—Judith Albright

6. Win – Win Outcomes

There are many ways to succeed on a short-term basis. If life was a three-day weekend, it wouldn't be hard to know what to do, and it wouldn't really matter any way. Life is a marathon and not a sprint.

Succeeding long-term is much different than becoming an overnight success. If you look behind the scenes of people who appear to be an overnight success, you will find that either their success came over many years and you weren't aware of it until recently, or the overnight success is really not successful.

For the sake of this exploration, I will briefly synthesize my own and many other definitions of success by saying that success are the ongoing pursuit of a worthwhile goal that fits our own passions and priorities.

If you succeed at doing something because everyone else wants you to do it while ignoring your own passion, you have failed. If you have instant success that is not sustainable, you have failed. And if your success does not bring success to others, you have failed.

There is no such thing as a win/lose outcome from a long-term perspective. You can cheat someone or take advantage of them and profit on a short-term basis; but you will never have an opportunity to do business with that person again, and the seeds you have planted in that transaction will bear bitter fruit. In a win/win transaction, both parties leave as a success and look forward to repeating the process.

My friend and colleague Zig Ziglar has become renowned for saying, "You can have everything in life you want if you'll help enough other people get what they want." This simple little statement captures the essence of a win/win relationship. Zig's statement causes you to instantly quit looking at your own potential success and look at the success of others.

Recently, I was negotiating the sale of many thousands of my books to a friend of mine who runs a major corporation for whom I have done a number of speeches. We discussed the price of the books, the availability of many thousands of copies, and several dozen delivery points throughout North America. I felt good about the negotiation and the resolution, and just as I was ready to conclude the deal, my friend asked a powerful question. "Is this deal good for you under the terms and conditions we have discussed?"

My friend is a shrewd businessman. He did not want to pay more money or receive fewer books, but he understands that unless we both win on this deal, there may not be another deal in the future, and that creates a lose/lose outcome for all concerned.

You cannot assume you understand what makes a relationship win/win for the other person. Unless you ask, you will simply be projecting your own goals and ambitions onto their situation.

As you go through your day today, find people and organizations whose success will make you successful, and you will begin to reap the long-term benefits of a win/win outcome.

Today's the day!

—Jim Stovall

7. The Upside-Down Way to Boost Your Motivation

You probably have some positive changes you'd like to make in your life—in your career, relationships, or health and fitness. You know that if you make those changes you will be happier and more successful.

So why aren't you already doing them?

Most of us have a pretty good idea of the steps we need to take to improve our lives. The real issue is overcoming inertia and taking the first step. Inertia tends to keep us in place, doing the same old things the same old way we've always done them.

We wait for motivation to arise and help us overcome inertia. We search for some hidden source of motivation deep inside us. We come to websites and read articles like this to learn new ways to develop greater motivation.

That's because we tend to look at the relationship between motivation and action this way:

Motivation ⟶ Action

And that's correct: Motivation does lead to action. If you feel motivated, you go out and do whatever it is you're motivated about.

But that's only part of the story. What too many of us forget is that the reverse is equally true: Motivation comes from having accomplished something.

When you have a sense of accomplishment, you are motivated to accomplish more. Basically, the more you get done, the more motivated you are to get things done.

Think back to a time in your life when you forced yourself to practice a new skill that you didn't enjoy—for one person it might be learning to swim, for another it might be public speaking. At first, as you struggled you were probably tempted to quit. But then you saw the result of all your efforts—you got to the end of the pool without sinking, or your audience laughed in all the right places and applauded you at the end. And suddenly you didn't have to force yourself to keep doing it, because now you wanted to.

Achievement feels good, so we naturally want to keep it up. That means the easiest and fastest way to get motivated to make a change in your life is to just start. Don't wait for motivation to arise—because you could be waiting forever. Get out there and do something, however small that something is. Once you accomplish it, your motivation will go up. And with greater motivation, you will get more done. And then your motivation will go up.

Pretty soon, you will have a self-feeding cycle of action and motivation. The inertia that was holding you back from living the life you want will be a thing of the past.

—***Tom Connellan***

8. Get Busy and Get Happy – In Defense of Busy Work

Busywork has a bad reputation. Keeping yourself (or someone else) busy doing meaningless or unnecessary task simply for the sake of avoiding idleness, a pointless waste of energy.

Recent research shows that keeping busy doing anything makes you a whole lot happier than you would have been doing nothing. Just sitting around, bored and inert, is a recipe for misery.

But if that's true, why then do we so often choose idleness? Why do we do nothing, when we could almost always be doing something?

The study of human behaviour is full of such paradoxes: People are happier when they do X. If you ask them, they'll even tell you they prefer to do X. Unfortunately, people often don't actually do X – they do The Opposite of X. And they have no idea why.

In this case, the answer seems to lie in our ability (or inability) to justify our actions. We really do prefer to be busy than to just sit around doing nothing, and being busy does in fact make us much happier, but we just can't bring ourselves to choose busyness over idleness without some sort of reason for the busyness.

A recent study, in which students were given the option of turning in a survey to get their candy reward in one of two places. They could turn it in right next door, though they would have to wait outside the door for 15 minutes before turning it in, or they could turn it in at another location that involved a 15 minute round-trip walk.

The majority of students chose to sit and wait next door, rather than take an unnecessary walk. They chose idleness over busywork (i.e., walking), despite the fact that the few who chose busywork reported being much happier when the 15 minutes were up.

But when the researchers introduced a justification for taking the long walk – that a different (though not actually better) candy would be offered as a reward for the walkers — the majority of students chose the busy option. "I really prefer the candy you get after the walk," they told themselves. But really, what they preferred was doing something over doing nothing, and all they needed was a reason. Any reason.

Two forces are usually at work whenever we do choose idleness. First, we have an aversion to needlessly expending energy. This aversion is probably built in to each of us as a part of our evolutionary inheritance.

Animals who waste the energy they need to find food and ward off predators are less likely to survive, so animals who spend their energy wisely have the survival advantage.

Second, human beings vastly prefer their actions to be meaningful. We like the things we do to have reasons — so much so that often when we don't really have a good reason for what we've done, we try to make one up. We are loathe to undertake any action when we know there is no justification for it.

The good news is, now that you know that busyness is better for you and will make you happier than just sitting around, you will always have a reason to choose busyness. Get up and do something. Anything. Even if there really is no point to what you are doing, you will feel better for it.

Incidentally, thinking deeply or engaging in self-reflection counts as keeping busy, too. You don't need to be running around; - you just need to be engaged, either physically or mentally.

As Victor Hugo once wrote, "A man is not idle because he is absorbed in thought. There is a visible labor and there is an invisible labor." Keep those mental wheels turning if you don't want to keep your feet moving.

—Heidi Grant Halvorson

Case Study

Now, I would like to share few case studies on motivation and expect my readers to analyze, interpret and solve the case based on their understanding and evaluation.

Motivation is a complex subject, although it seems very interesting to all of us, but it has many facets which hold different meanings for different people.

I have come across many incidents during my tenure as HR professional at various companies which are very complicated and are the result of some or the other conflict. Motivation has many theories written by different theorists, one such theory is reward and punishment theory also known as the theory X, and the other is carrot and stick theory. We will focus on theory X for the casestudy.

As a part of the company's Management Development Program, a group of managers from various functional areas have devoted several sessions to the study of motivation theory and the relevance of it in relation to the manager's responsibility of directing and controlling the operations of his organizational unit.

One of the participant is Rohit Sharma, who has been the supervisor of the production department from last one year. During his past this period he had no chance to attend any supervisory or developmental programs as he was attending the routine technical tasks.

The present plant manager has seen Rohit grow from an apprentice to a supervisor and is yet to reconcile with the change of responsibilities and designation of Rohit Sharma.

Rohit prepared the schedule on a particular day for all machines and a specific machine, which was on top priority. When Rohit came for his rounds he was surprised to find that the operator did not load the machine that was on the priority. Looking at this Rohit gets annoyed and the following conversation takes place:

Rohit to operator – Please do the job that is on priority.

Operator – Ther plant manager has given me another task after that I will take up your work.

Rohit – I don't want to hear anything, the plant manager has told me to stop everything else and take up the task on priority.

Operator – I have always done the task immediately whenever you have asked. But what about my increment which has been pending for over six months now.

Rohit - I'm not responsible for problems related to your increments, the top management manages such decisions on increment. I am helpless in this regard and suggest you go and sort this problem with plant manager.

Operator - As a supervisor it is your duty to solve my problem as I report to you.

Rohit – Please do not tell me my duties and if you will not do this work on priority now, I would report this incident as misbehaviour.

The operator threatend to go on strike and complained about the meagre salary and lack of increment.

Now during a session of motivation at the Management Development Program, Rohit made the following comments:

"Motivation theory makes sense in general, but there is no opportunity for us to apply these concepts in rear situations. After all our shop level employees are unionized and have job security. Motivation theories help me get the work done from my kids, but in a working environment we are working with adults and it seems to me this reward and punishment thing smacks of manipulation that just would not go over with people".

So, now it has become a complicated situation as Rohit does not seem to be interested in the motivational theories at all. Does the incident that happened between the operator and Rohit Sharma left such a mark in his mind that he started feeling threatened by unions and shop floor people?

Peoms that Motivate...

1. The world is against me

"The world is against me," he said with a sigh.
"Somebody stops every scheme that I try.
The world has me down and it's keeping me there;
I don't get a chance. Oh, the world is unfair!
When a fellow is poor then he can't get a show;
The world is determined to keep him down low."
"What of Abe Lincoln?" I asked. "Would you say
That he was much richer than you are to-day?
He hadn't your chance of making his mark,
And his outlook was often exceedingly dark;
Yet he clung to his purpose with courage most grim
And he got to the top. Was the world against him?"
"What of Ben Franklin? I've oft heard it said
That many a time he went hungry to bed.
He started with nothing but courage to climb,
But patiently struggled and waited his time.
He dangled awhile from real poverty's limb,
Yet he got to the top. Was the world against him?
"I could name you a dozen, yes, hundreds, I guess,
Of poor boys who've patiently climbed to success;
All boys who were down and who struggled alone,
Who'd have thought themselves rich if your fortune they'd known;
Yet they rose in the world you're so quick to condemn,
And I'm asking you now, was the world against them?"

—Edgar A. Guest

2. The road not taken

Two roads diverged in a yellow wood,
And sorry I could not travel both
And be one traveler, long I stood
And looked down one as far as I could

To where it bent in the undergrowth;
Then took the other, just as fair,
And having perhaps the better claim,
Because it was grassy and wanted wear;
Though as for that passing there
Had worn them really about the same,
And both that morning equally lay
In leaves no step had trodden black.
Oh, I kept the first for another day!
Yet knowing how way leads to way,
I doubted if I should ever come back.
Somewhere ages and ages hence:
Two roads diverged in a wood, and I
I took the one less travelled by,
And that has made all the difference.

—Robert Frost

3. Playing the game

Life is a game with a glorious prize,
If we can only play it right.
It is give and take, build and break,
And often it ends in a fight;
But he surely wins who honestly tries
(Regardless of wealth or fame),
He can never despair who plays it fair
How are you playing the game?
Do you wilt and whine, if you fail to win
In the manner you think your due?
Do you sneer at the man in case that he can
And does, do better than you?
Do you take your rebuffs with a knowing grin?
Do you laugh tho' you pull up lame?
Does your faith hold true when the whole world's blue?
How are you playing the game?
Get into the thick of it – wade in, boys!
Whatever your cherished goal;
Brace up your will till your pulses thrill,
And you dare – to your very soul!
Do something more than make a noise;
Let your purpose leap into flame
As you plunge with a cry, "I shall do or die,"
Then you will be playing the game.

—Unknown

4. It's the journey that's important

Life, sometimes so wearying
Is worth its weight in gold
The experience of traveling
Lends a wisdom that is old
Beyond our 'living memory'
A softly spoken prayer:
"It's the journey that's important,
Not the getting there!"
Ins and outs and ups and downs
Life's road meanders aimlessly?
Or so it seems, but somehow
Leads us where we need to be,
And being simply human
We oft question and compare...
"Is the journey so important
Or the getting there?"
And thus it's always been
That question pondered down the ages
By simple men with simple ways
To wise and ancient sages...
How sweet then, quietly knowing
Reaching destination fair:
"It's the journey that's important,
Not the getting there!"

—*John McLeod*

5. All for the best

Things mostly happen for the best.
However hard it seems to-day,
When some fond plan has gone astray
Or, what you've wished for most is lost
An' you sit countin' up the cost
With eyes half-blind by tears o'grief
While doubt is chokin' out belief,
You'll find when all is understood
That what seemed bad was really good.
Life can't be counted in a day.
The present rain that will not stop
Next autumn means a bumper crop.
We wonder why some things must be
Care's purpose we can seldom see

An' yet long afterwards we turn
To view the past, an' then we learn
That what once filled our minds with doubt
Was good for us as it worked out.
I've never know an hour of care
But that I've later come to see
That it has brought some joy to me.
Even the sorrows I have borne,
Leavin' me lonely an' forlorn
An' hurt an' bruised an' sick at heart,
An' though I could not understand
Why I should bow to Death's command,
That it was really better so.
Things mostly happen for the best.
So narrow is our vision here
That we are blinded by a tear
An' stunned by every hurt an' blow
Which comes to-day to strike us low.
An' yet some day we turn an' find
That what seemed cruel once was kind.
Most things, I hold, are wisely planned
If we could only understand.

—Edgar A. Guest

6. As you travel through life

As you travel through life there are always those times,
When decisions just have to be made,
When the choices are hard, and solutions seem scarce,
And the rain seems to soak your parade.
There are some situations where all you can do
Is simply let go and move on,
Gather your courage and choose a direction
That carries you toward a new dawn.
So pack up your troubles and take a step forward
The process of change can be tough,
But think about all the excitement ahead
There might be adventures you never imagined
Just waiting around the next bend,
And wishes and dreams just about to come true
In ways you can't yet comprehend!
Perhaps you'll find friendships that spring from new things
As you challenge your status quo,
And learn there are so many options in life,
Perhaps you'll go places you never expected

And see things that you've never seen,
Or travel to fabulous, faraway worlds
And wonderful spots in between!
Perhaps you'll find warmth and affection and caring
And somebody special who's there
To help you stay cantered and listen with interest
To stories and feelings you share.
Perhaps you'll find comfort in knowing your friends
Are supportive of all that you do,
And believe that whatever decisions you make,
They'll be the right choices for you.
So keep putting one foot in front of the other,
And taking your life day by day...
There's a brighter tomorrow that's just down the road –
Don't look back! You're not going that way!

—Unknown

7. Things work out

Because it rains when we wish it wouldn't,
Because men do what they often shouldn't,
Because crops fail, and plans go wrong
Some of us grumble all day long.
But somehow, in spite of the care and doubt,
It seems at last that things work out.
Because we lose where we hoped to gain,
Because we suffer a little pain,
Because we must work when we'd like to play
Some of us whimper along life's way.
But somehow, as day always follows the night,
Most of our troubles work out all right.
Because we cannot forever smile,
Because we must trudge in the dust awhile,
Because we think that the way is long
Some of us whimper that life's all wrong.
But somehow we live and our sky grows bright,
And everything seems to work out all right.
So bend to your trouble and meet your care,
For the clouds must break, and the sky grow fair.
Let the rain come down, as it must and will,
But keep on working and hoping still.
For in spite of the grumblers who stand about,
Somehow, it seems, all things work out.

—Edgar A. Guest

8. Be the best of whatever you are

If you can't be a pine on the top of the hill,
Be a scrub in the valley-but be
The best little scrub by the side of the rill;
Be a bush if you can't be a tree.
If you can't be a bush be a bit of the grass,
And some highway happier make;
If you can't be a muskie then just be a bass
But the liveliest bass in the lake!
We can't all be captains, we've got to be crew,
There's something for all of us here,
There's big work to do, and there's lesser to do,
And the task you must do is the near.
If you can't be a highway then just be a trail,
If you can't be the sun be a star;
It isn't by size that you win or you fail
Be the best of whatever you are!

—by Douglas Malloch

9. Profit from failure

The test of a man is the fight he makes,
The grit that he daily shows;
The way he stands on his feet and takes
Fate's numerous bumps and blows.
A coward can smile when there's naught to fear,
When nothing his progress bars;
But it takes a man to stand up and cheer
While some other fellow stars.
It isn't the victory, after all,
But the fight that a brother makes;
The man who, driven against the wall,
Still stands up erect and takes
The blows of fate with his head held high;
Bleeding, and bruised, and pale,
Is the man who'll win in the by and by,
For he isn't afraid to fail.
It's the bumps you get, and the jolts you get,
And the shocks that your courage stands,
The hours of sorrow and vain regret,
The prize that escapes your hands,
That test your mettle and prove your worth;
It isn't the blows you deal,

But the blows you take on the good old earth,
That show if your stuff is real.

—Unknown

10. Success

Success is speaking words of praise,
In cheering other people's ways.
In doing just the best you can,
With every task and every plan.
It's silence when your speech would hurt,
Politeness when your neighbor's curt.
It's deafness when the scandal flows,
And sympathy with others' woes.
It's loyalty when duty calls,
It's courage when disaster falls.
It's patience when the hours are long,
It's found in laughter and in song.
It's in the silent time of prayer,
In happiness and in despair.
In all of life and nothing less,
We find the thing we call success.

—Unknown

Conclusion

Booker T. Washington once said, "I have learned that success is to be measured not so much by the position that one has reached in life as by the obstacles overcome, while trying to succeed." The reason why you want to do something is **motivation.** It is an eagerness and willingness to do something without needing to be told or forced to do so." It encourages, inspires and develops a sense of pride, and builds self-esteem which is critical to productivity at a workplace.

According to an industry expert, "To build high motivation within yourself, determine your greatest motivator – is it money, incentives, bonus, commission, fame, recognition which are external and monetary benefits or non-financial motivators like pride, sense of achievement, responsibility, belief, challenging and interesting job, and respect, which are internal. Motivation however, comes from within. Keep smiling, be enthusiastic, cheerful and considerate; it is contagious. To boost your self-confidence, think win-win and not lose-lose.

Sir Winston Churchill has rightly said, "Kite rise highest against the wind, not with it." Failures and bounced back are elements of motivation. Failure is a learning tool that builds confidence. People with high self-confidence typically have little fear of unknown, are able to stand up for what they believe in and have the courage to risk embarrassment. Sri Chinmoy believes, "Your confidence need not be the result of your success. Your confidence can easily be the result of your implicit faith in tomorrow's most beautiful dawn." A man with motivation shall not lose, only doubt will bring defeat.

Dictionary is the only place where success comes before work. Hard work is the price we must pay for success. We can accomplish anything if we are willing to pay the price. If you're demotivated, it shows in your work, the way you manage customers, superiors and subordinates, that creates an unproductive, inefficient and pessimistic environment.

Encourage an environment where everyone encourages everyone else. Develop trust, respect, constructive criticisms and an open channel of upward and downward communication. Associate yourself with high motivators.

Enjoy yourself and find areas of interest at your workplace. Have a clear short and long-term goals. Be sober, kind, reliable and responsive. Know exactly what's expected from you and always meet your deadlines. As Richard Bach said, "The more I want to get something done, the less I call it work."

Finally, I would like to conclude with a short poem. Here it goes:

It couldn't be done

Somebody said that it couldn't be done,
but he with a chuckle replied
that "maybe it couldn't," but he would be one
who wouldn't say so till he'd tried.
So he buckled right in with the trace of a grin
on his face. If he worried he hid it.
He started to sing as he tackled the thing
that couldn't be done, and he did it.
Somebody scoffed: "Oh, you'll never do that;
At least no one ever has done it";
But he took off his coat and he took off his hat,
and the first thing we knew he'd begun it.
With a lift of his chin and a bit of a grin,
Without any doubting or quid it,
He started to sing as he tackled the thing
that couldn't be done, and he did it.
There are thousands to tell you it cannot be done,
there are thousands to prophesy failure;
there are thousands to point out to you, one by one,
the dangers that wait to assail you
But just buckle in with a bit of a grin,
Just take off your coat and go to it;
just start to sing as you tackle the thing
that "cannot be done," and you'll do it.

—*Edgar A. Guest*

Employee Motivational Questionnaire

1. Which factors in your organization motivates you?

____

____

2. Are there any obstacles that stops you from achieving your goals? If yes, what are they?

____

____

3. Do you have the required Authority and Power to perform your task? If No, what are the reasons?

____

____

4. Are there any negative factors in the company (like Director's resignation, union issues, recruitment freeze, etc) that is affecting your motivation level?

____

____

5. Does your organisation give you the opportunity to express your views, ideas or suggestions, and feedback?

____

____

6. Are they heard? If No, why?

____

____

7. Does your organization help employees grow and develop?

____

____

8. Do you feel safe, secure and protected in your organization?

____

____

9. Does your organization have a policy to handle employee grievances, problems and discontent?

____

____

10. Does your organization provide necessary training to improve your skills and competencies?

____

____

11. Have you ever faced any problem is motivating yourself at the work-place? If yes, please state some of the problems you have encountered?

____

____

12. How did you overcome these problems?

____

____

13. Rate the below mentioned Motivational factors on the scale of 1-15. (1 being the highest).

    i. Designation/Status.

    ii. Praise, Appreciation and Acknowledgement.

    iii. Job Security.

    iv. Bonus/ Incentives/ Allowances.

    v. Career Development.

    vi. Congenial Work Environment.

    vii. Employee participation in decision-making.

viii. Mutual Trust, Respect and Understanding.

ix. Independence/ Autonomy.

x. Flexible work hours.

xi. Training and Up gradation of skills.

xii. Interesting and Exciting work.

xiii. Recognition in Public.

xiv. Perfectionism.

xv. Fear of removal, demotion, transfer etc.

14. In addition to the above mentioned factors which other Motivational tool can be used to retain an employee?

____

____

Name of the organization: ______________________

Name of the respondent: ______________________

Designation: ______________________

THANK YOU

Employer Motivational Questionnaire

1. What is the Vision of your organization?

____

____

2. How you rate the attitude of your employees?

   o Motivating

   o Neither Motivating or Demotivating

   o Demotivating

3. According to you, what are the 5 major barriers that restrict employees from performing their best?

____

____

4. How you analyze the skill and ability of your employees?

   o Good.

   o Average.

   o Poor.

5. What Motivational tool you adopt to overcome such obstacles? (Rate the above on the scale of 1 to11. 1 being the highest)

   i. Challenging job.

   ii. Monetary benefits.

   iii. Flexible work hours.

   iv. Training and Development Opportunities.

   v. Vacations/Leaves/Holidays.

   vi. Recognition.

   vii. Autonomy and independence.

viii. Fair Promotion chances.

ix. Encouraging healthy competition.

x. Fostering team work.

xi. Job Security.

Any other, Please specify: ____________________

____

6. According to you what motivates your employees the most?

____

____

7. Do you think, Rewards (monetary and non-monetary) help to motivate your workplace and change their work attitude?

   o Always.

   o Sometimes.

   o Never.

8. How you rate your Management style?

   o Good.

   o Average.

   o Poor.

9. Is your work environment safe, convenient and hygienic?

   o Yes.

   o No.

10. Do you have the required amenities, facilities and services in your organization?

   o Yes.

   o No.

11. Do you allow your employees to share their ideas, views and suggestions?

   - o Always.
   - o Sometimes.
   - o Never.

12. Are your employees goal align with your organizational objectives?

   - o Always.
   - o Sometimes.
   - o Never.

Name of the organization: ______________________________

Name of the Respondent: ______________________________

Designation: ______________________________

THANK-YOU